F

The Golfer's Guide To The

AMERICAN SOUTHWEST

BRETT BORTON & THE EDITORS
OF WESTERN LINKS, THE "WHERE TO PLAY"
GOLF MAGAZINE

A FIRESIDE BOOK • Published by Simon & Schuster
New York London Toronto Sydney Tokyo Singapore

FIRESIDE
Simon & Schuster Building
Rockefeller Center
1230 Avenue of the Americas
New York, New York 10020

FIRESIDE and colophon are registered trademarks
of Simon & Schuster Inc.

Principal Photographer - Mike Klemme/Golfoto
Supervising Editors - Brett Borton, Mark Brown,
James Max Lane
Designed by Edward J. Cherry
Manufactured in the United States of America

10 9 8 7 6 5 4 3 2 1

Library of Congress Cataloging in Publication Data
is available.

ISBN: 0-671-74337-6

"What do we want with this vast, worthless area - this region of savages and wild beasts, of shifting sands and whirlwinds of dust, of cactus and prairie dogs? To what use could we even hope to put these great deserts and those endless mountain ranges?"

Daniel Webster

"A ball lying within a club length of a rattlesnake may be moved two club lengths without penalty."

Local Rule
Warren District Country Club
Bisbee, Arizona

Contents

Acknowledgments

The author wishes to thank the following people and organizations, without whom the successful completion of this book would not have been possible: The Arizona State Department of Library, Archives, and Public Records for the references to Dick Wick Hall's Salome Sun; Ed Gowan and Barry Palm of the Arizona Golf Association; Kevin Madden and John Hudak of Madden Publishing; Dan Poppers of David Hubbard for his invaluable contributions on Arizona golf; Parker Smith, who helped make my first trip to Arizona a memorable one; Dick Krull; Tracy Church of Loews Ventana Canyon Resort; Scott Johnson and Sally Hankin at the Metropolitan Tucson Convention and Visitors Bureau; Karen Oppenheim at La Quinta Hotel; Jim Wilmer and John Herndon at Westin Mission Hills Resort; Russ Pate and his Dallas friends for their permission to exploit their adventures at Marriott's Desert Springs; Mike Klemme for his usual stellar photography; Max Lane, Cindy Spaulding, Chris Duthie and Ed Cherry, my comrades at *Southern Links/Western Links*; everyone at Simon & Schuster for their patience; and finally, Sara, Jarrett and Haley, for hanging in 'til the bitter end.

Introduction

IT REPRESENTS PERHAPS THE great antithesis in golf, for nowhere else in the world has the game flourished on such spectacularly varied and strikingly beautiful terrain. Had the Scots ever seen land such as that of the Southwestern U.S., they would have never believed that their grand old game—a game founded along wind-swept linksland, set hard by the sea and fraught with a host of Mother Nature's own obstacles— could survive here. "It just doesn't bloody *belong* ...!" one such elder might say.

But it is because of this great contrast that golf thrives in the Southwest. In fact, Mother Nature couldn't have given golf architects a better canvas on which to dream. The light is sharp and vibrant, the air is dry and the landscape is unforgettable: lush deserts, rugged mountains and scarred canyons. It's a setting that demands creativity and conservation in equal measure. Set against the flaming reds, purples, browns, greens and

> "When you first see a desert course you want to bend down and touch the grass."

yellows of the desert, the bright fairways and greens of the golf courses seem like noble, mystical creatures of another world.

When you first see a desert course, all you want to do is bend down and touch the grass. In a land of the soaring and ancient saguaro cactus, the Gila monster and the desert bighorn sheep, the prickly pear and the ocotillo bush, the coyote and the roadrunner, the soothing contours of the fairway are an oasis for the eye and for the mind.

The measure by which golf has grown in the Southwest is equally unconventional. Despite the booming growth of golf in Arizona—some 220 golf courses statewide and counting, the highest number of courses per capita of any state west of the Mississippi—only in the past 10 years has the state effectively promoted itself as a world-class golf destination. On the other hand, Palm Springs and the surrounding Low Desert area of Southern California have been a favorite haunt for Hollywood celebrities, who began their escape to the region in the 1930s and brought golf with them shortly thereafter.

Then there's Las Vegas, the glitzy "Gateway to the West," where the green of the fairways nicely complements the hue of the gaming tables, and thus has to the little-known retreats. This is a region that, economically and culturally, has outgrown its image of sagebrush and cowboys and old mining towns, yet the land continues to serve as the thread that holds together this tapestry of time.

And like the land itself, golf in the desert is both spectacular and

become an integral by-product of the city's entertainment empire.

The purpose of "The Endless Fairway: Golf Courses of the Southwest" is to enlighten, entertain and educate readers on the rich bounty of great public-access golf that exists in this part of the country, from the five-star resorts intriguing, a test of one's ability as well as pure exhilaration for the senses. I've no doubt that the Scots would be pleased. A little confused, perhaps, but pleased.

Brett Borton - June 1992

Arizona

*The Greasewood Golf Lynx located at and around Salome, Arizona—
"Where She Danced"—and the Folks who See it All Say Nobody Saw
Nothing Like It Nowhere. The Course is Just a Little Over Twenty Three
(23) Miles Around and All Hazards & Bunkers are Natural—No
Artificial Ones Needed. Players are Warned to Use Maps and NOT to get
off the Far A Ways between the Holes. Good Guides Who Know the
Course can be Obtained at the BLUE ROCK INNE and Caddys and
Horses and Canteens, also Tents and Camping Outfits can be Leased by
the Week, Month or Season, Provided a Deposit is Put Up, and ALL
CADDYS AND HORSES LOST ON THE COURSE MUST BE PAID FOR.*

ACTUALLY, GOLF'S BEGINNINGS IN THE DESERT WEREN'T QUITE
as perilous as this 1927 account by Southwestern humorist Dick Wick
Hall. Writing in the old *Saturday Evening Post*, Hall imagined his
famous Greasewood course rolling across yawning canyons,
shimmering mirages and desolate ridges, with an average round taking
three days and approximately six-dozen balls. Hall counted a mesquite
thicket as a bunker, and a cow as a hazard—"and If She is Young and
Has a Calf, it's extra Hazardous. That's why our Caddys all go
horseback."

In reality, the desert's hot, rugged and dry character hardly made it a
suitable arena for a game invented for chill moor and fogbound
heather. Golf didn't reach the farm town of Phoenix until 1899—to a
hay field near where the State Fairgrounds is today. In the state's early
days of tourism, the game of choice was still "cowboys and Indians,"
and golf was never a part of the pitch. Arizonans were used to playing
on only a smattering of courses, many of which were laid out by
mining companies with fairways of alkali flats and greens of tamped
sand and oiled cottonseed.

Yet the Southwest was becoming somewhat of an international
attraction, and some pioneering hoteliers cultivated a more
sophisticated brand of Southwestern hospitality with oasis-like resorts
such as the Arizona Biltmore, San Marcos and The Wigwam. Early

guests were often respiratory patients shipped to the desert to convalesce in the dry heat. Once they caught their breath, they focused on their golf game. From their glowing reports, the word spread and, eventually, extended visits to Arizona no longer required a doctor's excuse. The Southwest became a winter haven, and golf was the hook.

Early desert designs by William Bell, Arthur Jack Snyder, Red Lawrence and Robert Trent Jones represented a more traditional slant to Arizona golf: a parkland feel with generous fairways often surrounded by trees 30 to 50 feet high. In the last decade, however, an ethic of respectful treatment of the desert has gained an expanded and influential following, fueled by legislation that limits the number of irrigatable acres per new golf course to just 90, and much less in some areas, versus 140 or more on existing courses. Thus began the evolution of desert or "target" golf, where players must carry arroyos, wash plains or small canyons to reach narrow fairways and undulating greens. Architects such as Pete Dye, Jack Nicklaus (who is credited with the first "target" golf course, Desert Highlands in Scottsdale), Tom Weiskopf and Jay Morrish, and Ted Robinson have since become pioneers in the continued growth of desert golf.

Today, golf is a significant cog in Arizona's economy, having ridden the coattails of the state's burgeoning tourism industry. Golfers alone generated $225 million for the state's coffers last year. Annual golf-related revenue exceeds the cash receipts from the state's dairy, cotton, and vegetable producers, and Arizona's golf-industry payroll easily surpasses many of its retail and service industries. All three major professional golf tours—the PGA, the Senior PGA and the LPGA—make regular stops in Arizona, and nearly every new resort hotel either has its own golf course or has access to a nearby facility. That turn-of-the-century skepticism about the game surviving in Arizona has vanished, much like an errant drive that strays from a lush manicured fairway into the untamed desert flora and fauna. With 320 days of sunshine annually, low humidity, settings that range from towering pine forests to arid desert floors, and a delightful mix of traditional and modern resorts, Arizona golf has truly come of age.

The Valley of the Sun

PHOENIX • SCOTTSDALE • MESA • TEMPE

Nowhere is desert golf more prominent than the "Valley of the Sun," a romantic (and eminently more marketable) designation for the Salt River Valley, encompasssing some 9,000 square miles across the low Sonoran Desert in southcentral Arizona. Encompassing the metro areas of Phoenix and Scottsdale as well as some 20 surrounding communities including Carefree, Mesa and Tempe, the Valley ranks as the 10th largest metropolitan area in the country. Yet nowhere else in Arizona is there such a contrast between urban sprawl and wilderness. More than half the state's population lives in the Valley of the Sun, but just beyond its borders lies craggy mountains, vast woodlands and seemingly endless desert. It is here where golf had its beginnings in Arizona, and it was the scene of dizzying development and construction in the mid-1980s, a period that made Arizona a world-class golf destination. Golf continues to flourish in the Valley, with more than 120 courses in the greater Phoenix/Scottsdale area alone.

Getting There

Phoenix Sky Harbor Airport is a thriving international airport serviced by 16 major airlines. All major rental car companies are represented, and there are bus connections to Phoenix as well as limousine service to virtually all major resorts in the area. The Scottsdale Municipal Airport is an outstanding full-service facility offering charter service to destinations in the U.S., Canada and Mexico as well as rental cars.

Weather

Summer in the Valley is hot; in fact, the mercury has been known to top out at 120 degrees on rare occasions. But it's a dry heat, and the low relative humidity makes the summers here bearable. So do the many off-season rates offered by the local resorts. Otherwise, the weather in the Valley is nothing short of perfect. The region's low

elevation keeps temperatures comfortably warm in the winter, aver-
aging 71 degrees during the day and 44 degrees at night. Spring and
autumn bring slightly warmer temperatures, ranging from the mid
'80s to the mid '50s. Rainfall is scarce (five to seven inches a year)
and usually occurs in July and August.

Activities

Outdoor activity is a way of life in the Valley of the Sun, and the
region's rich history and vast natural beauty lends itself to an array of
family-oriented adventures. For the truly adventurous, there's early
morning hot air balloon rides over the Valley, glider flights across the
Superstition Mountains, or river rafting over the white waters of the
Salt and Verde rivers. Each is a sheer delight for the senses. More
down-to-earth activities include horseback riding along the desert
trails, desert Jeep tours and gold panning expeditions in the Valley's
river canyons. To round out the day, try an authentic cowboy
barbecue, complete with a troubadour offering songs and tall tales
about life in the Wild West.

Attractions

The Phoenix/Scottsdale area is renowned for its museums and galleries. Among the best are the Heard Museum, the Phoenix Art Museum and the University Museum at Arizona State University in Tempe. The Heard features one of the country's best exhibits on native Americans, while the Phoenix Art Museum is the largest visual arts institution between Denver and Los Angeles. The Scottsdale Center for the Arts is a multimillion-dollar facility with five art galleries, an 800-seat theatre and a 2,500-seat amphitheatre, but a tour here should begin at the outdoor sculpture garden, a park-like setting showcasing the work of international and local artisans.

For a taste of the local history, try Pueblo Grande, the ruins of a town inhabited by the Hohokam Indians, who mysteriously disappeared in the 15th century; Pioneer Arizona, a dramatically authentic re-creation of an 1800s Western village set among rocky desert

foothills 30 miles north of Phoenix; or Rawhide, Scottsdale's version of a Wild West town complete with a saloon, stagecoach rides, period museums and exhibits, and some of the finest mesquite-broiled steaks and ribs this side of the Rockies. For more conventional entertainment, there's the Phoenix Cardinals of the NFL (September through December), the Phoenix Suns of the NBA (February through April), and college football's Sunkist Fiesta Bowl on New Year's Day at Sun Devil Stadium on the ASU campus. Kids will also enjoy the Phoenix Zoo, with more than 1,200 species spread over 125 acres of rolling hills.

Shopping

There's little here, or anywhere else for that matter, that can rival the Scottsdale Galleria, a glitzy $125-million specialty shopping and entertainment center that opened in 1991. In addition to an array of retail shops and restaurants, the center also features a seven-screen 2,000-seat movie complex and a one-million-gallon aquarium in the atrium where a tropical rain forest effect has been created. Also worth a visit in Scottsdale is El Pedregal, another relatively new complex with two levels of shops, galleries and restaurants with a strong Southwestern influence, and The Borgata, with 50 elegant boutiques set amidst narrow streets and courtyards reminiscent of an Old World Italian village. In Phoenix, the Biltmore Fashion Park is a luxurious array of 73 of the world's finest shops (Gucci, Saks, Elizabeth Arden, etc.) and restaurants. Even more intimidating, but on a much grander scale, is the Metrocenter, an Arizona landmark and the largest regional shopping center in the Southwest with more than 200 specialty stores.

Dining

Southwestern fare is the specialty here, obviously, but it's much more sophisticated these days. Try the enchilada stuffed with marinated duck, crab and cavier and you'll understand. While many of the larger resorts offer outstanding Continental and regional cuisine (which we will cover later) the Valley also offers a wide range of exemplary ethnic possibilities. For French cuisine, La Chaumiere in Scottsdale is both chic and cozy, while La Champagne at the Registry Resort, Scottsdale

has won numerous awards for its wine list and superb French Provencal cuisine. For Italian, there's Milano's, a charming country cottage with traditional favorites, or Prego Ristorante, a more trendy spot with very reasonable prices. Both are in Phoenix.

The best Chinese food in Phoenix is found at Hunan, with skilled chefs creating inpeccable Mandarin, Szechuan and Pekinese dishes. The *healthiest* Chinese food in Phoenix, and Scottsdale, is at China Gate, a family owned chain of three restaurants offering more than 200 items, from abalone to squid to tofu, with no MSG.

For More Information

- Phoenix & Valley of the Sun Convention & Visitors Bureau, 505 N. Second Street, Suite 300, Phoenix, AZ 85004-3998, (602) 254-6500.
- Scottsdale Chamber of Commerce, 7333 Scottsdale Mall, Scottsdale, AZ 85251-4498, (602) 945-8481.
- Tempe Convention & Visitors Bureau, 60 E. Fifth Street, Suite 3, Tempe, AZ 85281, (602) 894-8158.
- Mesa Convention & Visitors Bureau, 120 N. Center, Mesa, AZ 85201, (602) 969-1307.

Arizona Biltmore

The jewel of the desert

IT IS ONLY FITTING THAT ANY treatise on Arizona golf begin with the Arizona Biltmore, the "Grande Dame" of desert resorts and an international landmark. Tradition runs rampant throughout the resort's 39 lushly landscaped acres, and quality exudes from every corner. Managed by Westin Hotels and Resorts, the Biltmore's superb facilities, cuisine and service has made it a perennial Mobil Five-Star and AAA Five-Diamond award winner. It has been bestowed Five-Star status for 31 consecutive years, longer than any other U.S. resort.

Set in the foothills of Squaw Peak between Phoenix and Scottsdale, the Biltmore boasts more than 500 guest rooms and suites offering magnificent views in every direction. Its massive, manicured lawns give way to blankets of flowers. And everywhere, it seems, there are tributes to the legendary American architect, Frank Lloyd Wright. From the hotel itself, with its sandstone-colored block design, to the artwork and sculptures sprinkled liberally throughout the grounds, the Biltmore is a monument to his genius.

Wright figures most prominently in the resort's 62-year history. He collaborated with architect Albert Chase McArthur on the innovative design of the resort, using pre-cast concrete blocks that were molded on site and cast with exquisite detail and patterns. The "Biltmore Block" became the signature of the resort, which opened in February 1929 and immediately drew acclaim as the "Jewel of the Desert." A year later, on the heels of the stock market crash, the hotel and 1,200 acres of adjacent land were purchased by Chicago chewing gum magnate William Wrigley.

It was during Wrigley's 44 years of ownership that the Biltmore garnered international acclaim as a luxurious desert hideaway where the upper crust of society could relax or conduct business in the balmy Arizona winters. The clientele became legendary. Harpo Marx and his bride honeymooned at the Biltmore, and their lack of decorum—they reportedly held hands and skipped through the formal dining room after meals—both shocked and charmed fellow guests. Clark Gable once lost his wedding ring on the golf course (an employee recovered it). Spencer Tracy was a regular who became renowned for his tipping as well as his prowess at remembering the employees by name.

In June 1973 the Wrigley family sold the Biltmore to a company named Talley Industries. While closed for the summer season, the resort was undergoing the installation of a sprinkler system when a spark from a welding torch ignited insulation material. The fire destroyed the hotel's fourth floor, including its exquisite copper roof, and ruined the interior furnishings on the remaining floors. Immediately, the new owners commissioned Taliesin Associated Architects of the Frank Lloyd Wright Foundation to design and supervise the reconstruction of the damaged floors, as well as refurnish, refurbish and redecorate the remainder of the hotel. Incredibly, the reconstruction was completed in 82 days, and the hotel reopened for the winter season on September 29.

Ever since, the Frank Lloyd Wright Foundation has been mandated to maintain the architectural and interior design integrity of the Biltmore, which includes original Wrightian patterns, geometric designs and colors for the resort's furniture and carpeting. Subsequent renovations included these designs, and in 1987 six Wright sculptures—"The Biltmore Sprites"—were moved from Chicago's Midway Gardens, restored and recast, and placed around the grounds of the Biltmore.

The resort has changed hands several times since the Talley ownership, although Westin Hotels and Resorts of Seattle have managed the property since 1977. The current owners, Equitable Life Assurance Society of the United States, unveiled the first phase of a $20-million renovation in the fall of 1991 that brought back some of the hotel's original color schemes: sand and

The 36 holes of golf at the Arizona Biltmore represent two distinct eras in desert golf design.

gold accented by slate and copper. The result is a lighter, more spacious feel to the resort's common areas. The lobby, for instance, now evokes more of a "great hall" look, reminiscent of turn-of-the-century grand hotels. Another significant addition is the Lobby Lounge, where guests are afforded panoramic views of Squaw Peak.

The 36 holes of golf at the Biltmore represent two distinct eras in Arizona golf. The 60-year-old Adobe Course, designed by William Bell, is a throwback to the days when the issues of irrigatable acres and environmental preservation weren't in vogue. It is 6,900 yards of lush fairways, lakes and streams spread over 150 acres. While comfortable for players of average ability, Adobe's parallel fairways are lined with towering trees. A much higher premium is placed on the approach shots into small, well-bunkered greens. Adobe is truly an anomaly in the desert, for it represents one of only a handful of resort courses that retain the traditional parkland feel.

A more modern layout, yet still far removed from "target golf," is the Bill Johnston-designed Links Course at the Biltmore. Though some 500 yards shorter than Adobe, Links offers much tighter fairways spread over some unusually rolling terrain. In fact, several of the holes seem to be perfectly placed on the hillside of Squaw Peak, allowing for awesome views of the resort and nearby Phoenix.

The other Biltmore amenities are equally impressive. The newly renovated tennis complex offers 12 lighted courts, and nearby is the spacious Health and Fitness Center, with equipment and services comparable to some of the country's finest spas. Among the resort's three swimming pools is the round Catalina-tiled pool built by William Wrigley Jr. in 1930. Shuffleboard, croquet and volleyball are often contested on the resort's manicured lawns, and the bicycling and jogging path runs alongside the gently flowing Arizona Canal, one of several waterways dug by the extinct Hohokam Indians.

ARIZONA BILTMORE — PHOENIX, ARIZONA

LOCATION: 24th Street and Missouri, Phoenix, AZ 85016; 15 minutes from Sky Harbor Airport.

ACCOMMODATIONS: 502 guest rooms.

DINING/ENTERTAINMENT: Orangerie, award-winning contemporary cuisine; Gold Room Grille, art deco surroundings, breakfast, lunch and dinner; Cafe Sonora, casual, with Southwestern and American favorites; Cafe Sonora Patio, fireside cocktails on outdoor patio; Cabana Club and Pool Bar, poolside dining and cocktails; Lobby Lounge.

AMENITIES: 36 holes of golf; 12 lighted tennis courts; three swimming pools; health and fitness center; lawn games including shuffleboard, croquet and volleyball; jogging trails, biking and hiking;

MEETING FACILITIES: Conference Center with 39,000 square feet of meeting and banquet space, accommodates 12 to 1,250.

RATES: Standard rooms from $95.

RESERVATIONS: Call (602) 955-6600.

Dining at the Biltmore should be considered in the same context, for it is truly an exercise in culinary excellence. The resort's award-winning gourmet dining room, Orangerie, boasts the expertise of executive chef Peter Hoefler, who has also held court at the Plaza in New York, Chicago's Drake Hotel and the Hong Kong Hilton. Adventures in Orangerie begin with appetizers such as grilled duck sausage with sweet fennel and warm apple slaw, to an entree of potato-wrapped halibut with thyme and eggplant tomato caviar, followed by spiced applejack souffle with sandlewood ginger cream for dessert. Orangerie's wine room is equally stunning, with more than 6,000 bottles.

The Gold Room Grille offers mesquite-grilled steaks and seafood in a open, airy setting and a more moderate price range, along with live jazz in the adjoining lounge and a superb Sunday Brunch. Even more casual, yet no less

delectable, is Cafe Sonora and its Mexican and Southwestern regional specialties. Among the favorite dishes: Mexican bouillabaisse with poached seafood and shellfish, and yellow cornmeal pizza with smoked chicken, green onions, red and green tomato sauce and Mexican cheese.

Excellence and tradition—they are everywhere at the Arizona Biltmore, printed on the golf scorecards and instilled in every employee. Few resort properties can endure as many ownership changes and expansions, yet still retain the same allure and charm it possessed in 1929. Through it all, one objective has always prevailed, and it is on virtually every piece of printed material that the resort has ever produced. "With elegance and style, the highest standards of gracious innkeeping are to be maintained at all times..."

The philosophy works. The Arizona Biltmore just gets better with age. ∎

The Boulders

Capturing the romance of the desert

YOU HAVE TO LOVE A PLACE NAMED Carefree, where the streets have names like Never Mind Trail, Easy Street and Wampum Way, and you can loiter at the intersection of Ho and Hum. Snuggled into the Sonoran Desert foothills just north of Scottsdale, Carefree offers its residents a tranquil, unhurried existence for which their little corner of the world was named.

You don't have to live here, however, to share in the Carefree state of mind. Perched some 1,300 feet above Carefree, which itself is 2,500 feet above sea level, is The Boulders, a magnificent resort that perhaps best captures the stunning grandeur, as well as the intimate romance, of the desert.

Those who have visited The Boulders will attest to the fact that the resort is virtually impossible to fault. One rather fitting testimonial comes from *Andrew Harper's Hideaway Report*, a monthly newsletter that updates its subscribers (average income: $302,000) on America's "peaceful and unspoiled places." Its readers annually rank the country's top luxury resorts, and for the last four years The Boulders has come out on top.

It is a $50-million resort, but there is no trace of glitz or pretentiousness here. The entire development was designed to blend in with the natural surroundings of the high Sonoran Desert and the 12-million-year-old granite boulder formations that dot the landscape. Its guest rooms, individual adobe-colored casitas, are scattered like a broken strand of pearls along the boulder-strewn landscape, guarded by towering cacti, vivid wildflowers and a host of jackrabbit, hawk and deer.

"There is a true spirit of romance here that is hard to describe in words or pictures," said William Nassikas, vice president and general manager of The Boulders and a partner in Westcor Resorts, which manages the property. "This is more than a resort.... it's an experience. It's the scent of burning juniper wood in the fireplaces and desert sunsets. Most of all, it's a sense of serenity."

The Boulders originally opened in 1969 as a small golf and residential community and operated as such throughout the 1970s with a pair of nine-hole courses designed by Red Lawrence and Arthur Jack Snyder. Westcor Partners, a group of successful Southwestern businessmen, acquired the entire project in the early 1980s and immediately began transforming the sleepy hamlet into a world-class resort destination. A new main building and clubhouse were added, and Jay Morrish, then associated with Jack Nicklaus' Golforce design outfit, was brought in to overhaul the golf courses. He created three new nine-hole courses—Lake, Saguaro and Boulders—and golf at The Boulders soon became renowned not only for its unrequited beauty, but for its overt intimidation as well. "Desert golf," as it were, was still a relatively new concept, and the uninitiated found it rather shocking to encounter 300-year-old saguaros growing smack in the middle

of bunkers and "rough" taking the form of the Sonoran Desert, instead of the more traditional tall grass, trees and bushes. Cacti and rattlesnakes brought new meaning to the word "hazard."

Indeed, few golf courses in America can be as exhilarating and as difficult as the rota at The Boulders. The resort opened a fourth nine in the fall of 1991, yet another Morrish creation, which in turn created The Boulders North (the old Saguaro and Lakes courses) and The Boulders South (eight original holes and two reconstructed holes from the Boulders nine, and eight completely new holes). By retaining Morrish as the

Golf at The Boulders is renowned for its uncompromising beauty and its overt intimidation.

architect, the resort has maintained a consistency of character that makes such a transformation plausible.

And any doubt as to whether the new holes measure up is quickly resolved at the first hole of Boulders South: from the elevated tee box of this 440-yard par-four, golfers view the resort's "signature" boulder pile towering over the main lodge and casitas to the south, with Chimney Rock and Black Mountain rising in the distance. The breathtaking view sets the tone for the entire round.

Things have been equally idyllic for Westcor, which has built upon its enormous success at The Boulders with two other thriving desert resorts: Westcourt in the Buttes in nearby Tempe, and the

THE BOULDERS — CAREFREE, ARIZONA

LOCATION: 34631 North Tom Darlington Drive, Carefree, AZ 85377; 16 miles northeast of Phoenix; 33 miles from Sky Harbor Airport; 13 miles from Scottsdale airport.

ACCOMMODATIONS: 136 guest casitas

DINING/ENTERTAINMENT: The Latilla, formal dining; the Palo Verde Room, regional specialties; the Boulders Club, lunch and dinner; the Discovery Lounge, nightly entertainment; the Bakery Cafe; and Cantina del Pedregal.

AMENITIES: 36 holes of golf designed by Jay Morrish; six plexi-cushioned tennis courts; a fitness center with exercise equipment and aerobics classes, lap pool and Jacuzzi.

MEETING FACILITIES: The Sonoran Ballroom, 2,000 square feet accommodating up to 200.

RATES: From $210 to $570.

RESERVATIONS: Call (602) 488-9009; or (800) 553-1717.

Hotel Westcourt in northwest Phoenix. Westcor's corporate philosophy dictates that its resorts be situated on unusual sites with unique physical character. The Boulders fits the bill, with a meticulous master plan that flows through the intrinsic beauty of the high Sonoran. Westcor also demands outstanding service from its employees and, with The Boulders, there's no argument to be made here. Resort guests enjoy a service level more suited to a private club: highly personalized and infinitely accommodating.

Other amenities are equally impressive. The casitas are among the most uniquely luxurious of any American resort, with Southwestern-flavored furnishings and artifacts, wood-beamed ceilings, wood-burning fireplaces and private patios affording extraordinary views.

The resort recently added a $3.7-million fitness center emphasizing a natural approach combining aerobics, flexibility exercises and hiking (using llamas as pack animals) or biking in the desert. Guests may also choose from five excellent restaurants, the most noteworthy being the elegant Latilla Room, with formal dining overlooking a cascading waterfall and the massive rock formation that inspired the resort's name.

Take it from the readers of the *Hideaway Report*: The Boulders is as peaceful and unspoiled as it gets, capturing the romance of the desert perhaps better than any other Southwestern property. So relax and enjoy, and if you should encounter any uneven lies on the golf course, remember that everything breaks toward Phoenix. ∎

Hyatt Regency Scottsdale

A sparkling symbol of the desert's modern era

IT IS, IF YOU'LL PARDON AN ALREADY overused cliche, an oasis; a shining jewel in the midst of a barren environment that at one time seemed to defy any notion of successful development. A sea of deep green fairways and sparkling blue lagoons, colorful gardens and splashing waterfalls and crackling fireplaces, the Hyatt Regency Scottsdale perhaps best represents the model of tasteful modern-era resort development in the Arizona desert.

It is also the continuance of a successful marriage between man and nature in this little corner of Scottsdale. The Hyatt Regency Scottsdale is the resort hub of Gainey Ranch, a 640-acre resort and residential community that offers 27 holes of outstanding golf, miles of walking and jogging trails through the Sonoran foothills, and an abundance of greenspace (more than 40 percent of the total acreage). The site is the former homestead and working ranch of Daniel C. Gainey, a self-made millionaire, renowned horse breeder and outdoorsman extraordinaire who moved his family to Scottsdale from Minnesota in the early 1950s.

Gainey's legacy of environmental stewardship is the driving force behind the development of Gainey Ranch, and the philosophy is perpetuated in dramatic fashion by the Hyatt Regency Scottsdale. As guests enter the lobby they are greeted by an 820-square-foot moveable glass wall that highlights the panoramic view of the desert and McDowell Mountains. The grounds resemble a 27-acre garden with acres of waterways, an abundance of fountains and waterfalls, and hundreds of palms, fir trees, hanging plants and flowers. An international art collection is spread around the resort, a variety of distinctive displays that range from the historical to the whimsical, yet all of which respond to the grand scale of the landscape.

Blending beautifully within these lush surrounds is the 27-hole Gainey Ranch Golf Club, three distinctively different nine-hole tracks that offer some of the best resort golf in the Valley of the Sun. Designer Mike Poellot, a former associate of Robert Trent Jones Jr., describes the Arroyo, Lakes and Dunes courses as "a series of choices, with a relatively 'safe way' or a 'challenging way'...with the appropriate rewards and penalties." In other words, with four pin positionings on each hole, the courses can be as playable or as testing as one desires.

The Arroyo Course, the longest (at 3,424 yards) and the most open of the three nines, takes both its name and chief features from the natural drainage routes which traverse the Gainey Ranch property. Enhanced by the use of native flowering plants and boulders, the course is perhaps most reminiscent of a true Southwestern course. On the other hand, the Dunes Course (3,238 yards) encompasses a more Scottish feel, with dramatically rolling sand dunes— played as natural hazards, not traps— ridges, knolls and valleys.

As the "showcase" nine, the Lakes Course (3,376 yards) offers its challenge by way of strategically located lakes, ponds, streams and waterfalls. In addition to its visual appeal, the Lakes Course also addresses many of the irrigation and flood control requirements of the site, with the water hazards accommodating excess water from winter rains and providing an irrigation base during the dry summer months.

Water is an integral part of the Hyatt Regency Scottsdale's other signature amenity, a $3.8-million, half-acre "water playground" which includes a three-story waterslide inside a clocktower, a children's pool complete with a sand beach, and the "Big Gun," a thundering waterfall pumping 600 gallons of water per minute.

The Gainey Ranch Golf Club offers three distinctively different nines with an abundance of water.

The resort's other recreational offerings are somewhat less imposing—there's tennis, the Regency Spa health club, and the aforementioned jogging and cycling trails that wind throughout the Gainey Ranch community. Desert Jeep tours and horseback riding can be arranged through the hotel concierge.

Accommodations are attractively varied and, in the Hyatt Regency tradition, quite elegant. There are 477 rooms and suites in the hotel's main building, all offering private balconies with water, courtyard, golf course or mountain views. On either side of the main building are seven free-standing casitas, available in two- or four-bedroom configurations, with terraced balconies overlooking a lake. The hotel's Regency Club, an exclusive wing on the third floor, offers personal concierge service and daily food and beverage servings, and special in-room amenities.

Since its opening, the Hyatt Regency Scottsdale has scored several hospitality industry awards for excellence; most notably, AAA Four-Diamond and Mobil Four-Star designations, and the "Family Resort of the Year" award for 1991 from *Family Circle* magazine.

The Hyatt has been named one of the top ten meeting facilities in the U.S., with 37,000 square feet of both indoor and outdoor space, and its elegant Golden Swan restaurant—one of three fine dining rooms on property—has been a *Travel/Holiday* "Outstanding Restaurants of the World" honoree for several consecutive years. The Hyatt's culinary staff has won numerous awards in regional and international competition.

No wonder, then, that the Hyatt Regency Scottsdale is considered one of the flagship hotels among Hyatt's resort properties. Yet, like Scottsdale itself, the Hyatt is elaborate without being excessive, and elegant without being stuffy. In an era when modern resort development has tended to favor glitz and glamour over form and function, that speaks volumes. ■

HYATT REGENCY SCOTTSDALE — SCOTTSDALE, ARIZ.

LOCATION: 7500 East Doubletree Ranch Road, Scottsdale, AZ 85258; approximately 25 minutes from Phoenix Sky Harbor Airport.

ACCOMMODATIONS: 493 guest rooms on four floors; 25 suites; one- and two-story casitas.

DINING/ENTERTAINMENT: Golden Swan, award-winning regional American cuisine; Squash Blossom, Southwestern-influenced fare for breakfast, lunch and dinner; Ristorante Sandolo, casual Italian cafe with singing waiters and sandolo boat rides; The Lobby Bar, cocktails with nightly entertainment.

AMENITIES: 36 holes of golf; tennis; swimming; 25,000-square-foot European spa; horseback riding; desert Jeep tours.

MEETING FACILITIES: 28,000 square feet of indoor meeting space including 14,000-square-foot Regency Ballroom with banquet space for 1,200; theatre-style seating for 1,550.

RATES: Standard guest rooms from $115; Regency Club rooms from $175. Casitas from $550.

RESERVATIONS: Call (602) 991-3388.

Marriott's Camelback Inn

Where time stands still

IT'S EARLY EVENING IN PARADISE Valley, just west of Scottsdale. A perfumed breeze gently ruffles the palms overhead as shadows lengthen across the emerald lawns. The sunset once again promises to be spectacular. It's the close of another perfect day at the venerable resort where time really does seem to stand still.

It is Marriott's Camelback Inn, and for 56 years it has represented the epitome of Southwestern style and charm. Camelback indulges its guests in a level of gracious hospitality that makes it a regular recipient of both the Mobil Five-Star and AAA Five-Diamond awards. Its setting, 125 magnificently landscaped acres at the foot of Camelback and Mummy Mountains, has made it one of the desert's premier destinations since 1936.

True, while "where time stands still" remains an appropriate motto for the Camelback Inn, progress has greatly enhanced the resort's lofty standards of excellence. The single most important event in the Inn's storied history—save perhaps for founder Jack Stewart's efforts at securing the financing needed to build the resort in 1936—was its

purchase by the Marriott Hotel Corporation in 1967. In the past four years, Marriott has reinvested more than $14 million in the resort as part of its "Grand Plan," a massive four-phase refurbishment effort to maintain Camelback's stellar reputation in the valley.

One phase of the Grand Plan involved the creation of a magnificent 23,000-square-foot spa that rivals any such facility in the Southwest. As expected, the Spa at Camelback offers a variety of fitness facilities and services, body and beauty treatments, and wellness programs. What sets this one apart is its association with the Dallas-based Institute of Aerobic Research and its founder, Dr. Kenneth H. Cooper, the father of the aerobic concept. This is as close as you can get to a *real* aerobic workout, followed perhaps by a seaweed mud body wrap and an outdoor massage at the foot of Mummy Mountain. It's as exhilarating for your mind as it is for your body.

But perhaps the grandest phase of the Grand Plan was its room enhancement program, the single most comprehensive upgrade in the history of the resort. Three years in the making, it in-

volved the complete refurbishing and redecorating of all 425 guest casitas to better reflect the history and style of the Southwestern culture. Everything from the cabinetry to the cocktail tables were custom made; Marriott officials reportedly made a trip to the furniture maker in California to make sure there were enough stress marks and worm holes in the wood. As the *coup de grace*, the works of local artisans were incorporated into the plan to ensure authenticity.

Yet while Camelback guests may *feel* as if they're in old Arizona, a few modern in-room amenities such as honor bars, automatic coffee makers and telephone systems with computer and fax hookups will comfortably rouse them back to reality. There are also 23 elegant and expansive suites, seven of which have their own private pools.

Despite all of its capital improvements, a legacy of exemplary service is still Camelback's calling card. Again, Marriott is a key player. Consistency of service is a common thread of every Marriott facility, particularly in its burgeoning golf operations. The so-called "Marriott Way"—a philosophy of treating resort guests to a golf "experience," the sum of several individual experiences rather than a succession of golf shots—was pioneered here.

First, a little background on Camelback's golf courses. The resort's 36 holes represent pure resort golf: scenic and well-maintained, challenging when played from the tips but otherwise

The epitome of Southwestern charm and gracious hospitality, the Camelback Inn has been one of the desert's premier destinations since 1936.

eminently playable. You will never see a major tournament here, but you won't pay $100 and lose a dozen balls, either.

Camelback's Padre Course, a Red Lawrence design which plays 6,559 yards to a par of 71, offers tight fairways framed by stands of pine and eucalyptus and medium-sized, elevated greens. But water comes into play only twice—and even then it is not particularly threatening—there are no forced carries off the tee, and while the greens are well-bunkered, there are openings in front for run-up shots.

The Indian Bend Course, designed by Arthur Jack Snyder and opened in 1978, is better suited to the power hitter. A links-style layout with nine holes playing out and nine coming back, Indian Bend is longer (7,014 yards, par 72) but more wide open. The terrain offers a bit more undulation than on Padre, but there is little water and much less tree cover with which to contend. If you can get past the first hole, a 432-yard dogleg left and the course's No. 1 handicap hole, Indian Bend is quite manageable.

Shortly after Camelback began offering golf to its guests in the early 1970s, a fellow by the name of Roger Maxwell assumed the helm as director of golf. While certainly no slouch at the game, Maxwell's real strength was in merchandising. Tapping into his previous experience with Saks Fifth Avenue, he initiated a policy of buying narrow and deep, mixing the subtle with the sizzling and the practical with the provocative. As a result, the Camelback Golf Shop developed a steady stream of regular, highly discriminating buyers and established itself as one of the finest golf shops in the world.

MARRIOTT'S CAMELBACK INN — SCOTTSDALE, ARIZ.

LOCATION: 5402 E. Lincoln Drive, Scottsdale, AZ 85253; approximately 20 minutes north of Phoenix Sky Harbor Airport.

ACCOMMODATIONS: 423 casitas; 23 suites.

DINING/ENTERTAINMENT: Chapparal Dining Room, award-winning Continental fare; The Navajo Room, Southwestern surroundings; Dromedary's, light fare poolside; Sprouts, health-conscious breakfast and lunch; Oasis Lounge; 19th Hole; Chapparal Lounge.

AMENITIES: 36 holes of golf; tennis; swimming; 25,000-square-foot European spa; horseback riding; desert Jeep tours.

MEETING FACILITIES: 40,000 square feet of meeting and banquet space including 16,000-square-foot Arizona Ballroom.

RATES: Standard rooms from $95.

RESERVATIONS: Call (800) 228-9290 or (602) 948-1700.

The operation continues to thrive under director of golf Joe Shershenovich; Maxwell has since moved on to oversee operations for Marriott's 17 golf facilities throughout the U.S. and Bermuda.

The "Marriott Way" also carries over to the golf staff which, in season, is the largest in the nation with 25 golf professionals. Scheduling a lesson is rarely a problem here, and you won't find a more gracious group of instructors. In fact, the entire resort staff, from the housekeepers to the servers at

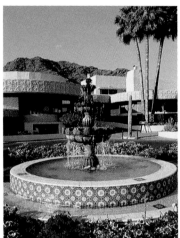

Camelback's highly regarded Chapparal Dining Room, are well versed in the art of guest service. It's the cornerstone of the partnership between Camelback and Marriott, and the result is a model of resort management.

"Everywhere I've worked in the Valley, we've been told, 'Do it like Camelback does,'" said head golf professional Mark Bakeman. "People would tell me, 'If you have a chance to go anywhere, go to Camelback.'"

Our sentiments exactly. ∎

The Phoenician

The High Princess of desert grandeur

LONG BEFORE ITS OPENING IN October 1988, The Phoenician was destined to be different from other Valley of the Sun resort hotels. For starters, it was the brainchild of Charles Keating, the dubious California savings and loan magnate and junk bond salesman who these days hangs his hat in a resort of a different ilk. The hotel was developed with unbridled extravagance (a monument to Keating's heyday in the Reagan '80s) and has been widely criticized as being ostentatious to the point of tackiness. It was indeed unlike anything in these parts, from its $6-million-plus art collection to its two-acre cactus garden to its lifesized outdoor chess board.

But as a wise man once said, wretched excess does have its place in this world, and anyone who is overly critical of The Phoenician has probably never been a guest there. With luxurious appointments, expansive accommodations and impeccable amenities and service, The Phoenician offers a guest experience that is unrivaled. A AAA Four-Diamond designee, The Phoenician was voted by readers of *Condé Nast Traveler* in 1991 as No. 2 of the top 20 mainland resorts in the U.S., and the United Kingdom's *Harper's & Queen* named it one of the top 100 hotels in the world. Despite the lambasting that The Phoenician has taken over the years—much of it, admittedly, from its Keating connection—they're obviously doing something *very* right.

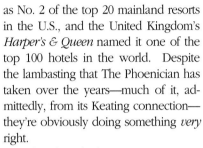

With a breathtaking setting on 130 acres at the base of Camelback Mountain, The Phoenician enjoys an attractive location midway between Phoenix and Scottsdale. Each of its 473 guest rooms offers 600 square feet of space with rattan furniture, wool Berber carpeting, oversized marble baths, three telephones (each with two lines plus a dedicated line for a personal computer modem), the *de rigueur* honor bar, and 27-inch remote control stereo television. Those requiring additional privacy, or making longer stays, may choose a lakefront casita with fireplace, walk-in closets and full kitchen.

There are three distinctive restaurants within the resort—the elegant Mary Elaine's offers a superb wine list—and the amenities are exemplary as well.

The Phoenician's Tennis Garden, with 11 lighted courts, has been given the highest rating by the sport's major publications, and the resort's oval pool (an aquatic showpiece tiled in mother-of-pearl) is one of seven swimming pools interconnected by a series of cascading waterfalls. There's also the Centre for Well Being, where basic fitness and general pampering give way to a complete overhaul of body and mind. Herbal wraps and brow tinting have never been this luxurious.

There are certainly more challenging golf courses in the valley than the Homer Flint-designed 18 holes at The Phoenician, but a more immaculately maintained track may not exist. While the front nine is more traditional—a series of lush fairways with minimal bunkering and a smattering of water hazards—the back nine takes golfers up and down the side of Camelback Mountain. Playing nearly 300 yards longer, the incoming nine pars at 37 and offers three particularly entertaining par-fives: the potential two-shot 16th (487 yards) and the no-way-in-hell 14th and 18th (588 and 520 yards, respectively). With a slope rating of 134, the course is by no means a pushover. But with its delightful mix of palms and orchids with Saguaro and desert bramble, it's more of an aesthetic wonderland that's perfectly suited for resort guests.

Actually, The Phoenician probably

Camelback Mountain casts an imposing shadow over The Phoenician and its 18-hole golf course.

garners as much attention for its land-scaping as its lavish interior appoint-ments. A maintenance staff of 25 over-sees the golf course alone; another 40 full-time landscapers maintain the lawns, flower gardens, trees, shrubs, and the aforementioned Cactus Gar-den, where resort guests can learn about the indigenous wildlife and veg-etation of the Sonoran Desert. Hey, who says you can't be swathed in ex-travagance and be enlightened at the same time?

As guests at The Phoenician dis-cover, just about anything is possible here. ∎

THE PHOENICIAN — SCOTTSDALE, ARIZONA

LOCATION: 6000 East Camelback Road, Scottsdale, AZ 85251; nine miles north of Phoenix Sky Harbor Airport.

ACCOMMODATIONS: 473 guest rooms and suites in main hotel; 107 lakefront casitas including 12 parlor suites.

DINING/ENTERTAINMENT: Mary Elaine's, gour-met dining; Terrace Dining Room, Italian-American cuisine; Oasis, poolside fare; Win-dows on the Green; Charlie Charlie's, popular night spot with club-like atmosphere; The Praying Monk, wine cellar room for intimate dining; 19th Hole; Cafe & Ice Cream Parlor.

AMENITIES: 18 holes of golf; 11 lighted tennis courts; croquet lawn; seven swimming pools; Centre for Well-Being; children's program.

MEETING FACILITIES: 60,000 square feet of space including 22,000-square-foot ballroom, a business center and a multi-media theatre.

RATES: Standard hotel rooms and casita bedrooms from $145; one-bedroom suites from $725; two-bedroom suites from $1,050. Golf, tennis, and fitness packages from $519.

RESERVATIONS: Call (800) 888-8234 or (602) 947-4311.

The Pointe Resorts

Spreading the wealth throughout the valley

REMEMBER THE GREAT SCENE IN "Butch Cassidy and the Sundance Kid," when Butch, exasperated by the pursuit by the mysterious man in the straw hat and his posse, asks Sundance, "Who *are* those guys?" One who doesn't hail from the Southwest might ponder the same about Gosnell Builders, the development firm responsible for the expansive Pointe Resorts in Phoenix.

They're not Disney or Arvida or Westinghouse, but Gosnell's track record in quality resort, residential and commercial construction is indeed impressive. Founded in 1973 and headquartered in Phoenix, Gosnell owns and operates several commercial properties in Arizona and Southern California in addition to its real estate development and construction business. To date, the company boasts completed projects valued in excess of $2 billion.

On the resort side, the company's most ambitious projects are The Pointe Resorts, three full-service interactive properties located in the heart of the Valley of the Sun. The trio—Squaw Peak and Tampatio Cliffs to the north of Phoenix, and South Mountain to the south—are characterized by striking Spanish Mediterranean architecture, picturesque mountain parks, tropical courtyards, comfortably appointed suite accommodations and an array of fine amenities, including golf.

The Pointe at Squaw Peak is sited on 300 acres adjacent to the 3,000-acre Phoenix Mountain preserve. It offers 576 suites and 78 one- and two-bedroom villas; more than 44,000 square feet of meeting space; five restaurants (highly recommended: the casual eatery, Beside the Pointe, and its adjacent sports bar) with fare ranging from traditional Southwestern to innovative Northern Italian; six swimming pools; eight lighted tennis courts and four indoor racquetball courts; and a fully equipped fitness center. Just minutes away is the Pointe at Tampatio Cliffs, a $300-million resort village perched along the cliffs of the Phoenix North Mountains. Tampatio Cliffs is noted for its superb accommodations (600 suites spread along lush terraces and winding lanes) and its restaurants, particularly Entienne's Different Pointe of View. With a breathtaking mountaintop setting overlooking Phoenix, Entienne's elegant surroundings and fine French cuisine has been recognized by *Travel/Holiday* and *Phoenix* magazine, which named it the city's best restaurant for three consecutive years.

For golf, guests at Squaw Peak and Tampatio Cliffs play The Pointe Golf Club at Lookout Mountain, a 6,617-yard course designed by Bill Johnston.

The former site of the Senior PGA Tour's Arizona Classic, Lookout Mountain is a rolling and picturesque desert mountain layout that plays over craggy ravines and desert washes. The holes—a unique combination of five par-3s, eight par-4s, and five par-5s—are bordered by Saguaro cacti and, in some areas, offer panoramic views of the Phoenix Valley.

Another admirable quality is that the four tee settings offer a tremendous variance in playability. Two prime examples: The par-three sixth hole can stretch from 132 yards to a downright ugly 248, while the par-five 18th stretches from 383 to 512 yards.

Below and right: The Pointe Golf Club at Lookout Mountain has hosted a Senior PGA Tour event.

The newest of the Pointe resorts is The Pointe on South Mountain, located 10 minutes south of downtown Phoenix on Interstate 10. In addition to more than 600 well-appointed suites, South Mountain is renowned for its Sports Club, a 40,000-square-foot, three-level facility with 10 lighted tennis courts, five racquetball courts, an astounding array of exercise equipment (Nautilus, Keiser, Eagle, LifeCycle, StairMaster, etc.), aerobics programs, and a beauty and hair salon.

The newest addition to the South Mountain Sports Club is the 6,400-yard Pointe on South Mountain Golf Club, a layout that favors accuracy and proper club selection over power. Set on just 90 acres, the course offers three distinct looks; the first six holes take on an uncharacteristic tropical feel, highlighted by nine water hazards; holes 7 through 12 are characterized by natural outcroppings of rock and native vegetation for a narrow, target golf appearance; and the last six holes are designed around the dramatic elevation changes afforded by the nearby mountain range.

Designed by Forrest Richardson and Arthur Jack Snyder, South Mountain offers four sets of tee boxes (in some cases five) to accommodate virtually every skill level.

Since their inception in 1977, The Pointe Resorts have garnered virtually every major award offered to the hospitality industry, from the AAA Five-Diamond to the Pinnacle Award for outstanding meeting facilities from *Successful Meetings* magazine. So much for a lack of recognition. ■

THE POINTE RESORTS · PHOENIX, ARIZONA

LOCATION: The Pointe at Squaw Peak: 7677 North 16th Street, Phoenix, AZ 85020. The Pointe at Tampatio Cliffs: 11111 North 7th Street, Phoenix, AZ 85020. The Pointe on South Mountain: 7777 South Pointe Parkway, Phoenix, AZ 85044.

ACCOMMODATIONS: Squaw Peak: 576 suites and 78 one- and two-bedroom villas. Tampatio Cliffs: 600 suites. South Mountain: 640 suites.

DINING/ENTERTAINMENT: Squaw Peak: Inauzzi Pointe of View, Northern Italian cuisine in casual elegant setting for dinner and Sunday brunch; Beside The Pointe, casual breakfast, lunch and dinner fare (salads, omelettes, sandwiches, etc.) in garden setting; Hole-in-the-Wall, "cowboy cuisine," i.e. mesquite-grilled steaks, ribs, etc., in rustic setting; Aunt Chilada's, authentic Mexican entrees for lunch and dinner in colorful atmosphere.

Tampatio Cliffs: Entienne's Different Pointe of View, award-winning gourmet cuisine and vintage wines in mountaintop setting; Pointe in Tyme, turn-of-the-century decor with signature items from the country's finest restaurants for breakfast, lunch and dinner; Waterin' Hole, hearty Western fare in jovial, honky-tonk setting for lunch and dinner.

South Mountain: Another Pointe in Tyme, spin-off of sister restaurant at Tampatio Cliffs with breakfast, lunch and dinner; Beside The Pointe, same as Squaw Peak location with casual fare for breakfast, lunch and dinner in garden setting; Rustler's Roost, Western fare for lunch and dinner with live country music and mountaintop setting overlooking Phoenix; Aunt Chilada's, same as Squaw Peak location with Mexican fare for lunch and dinner.

AMENITIES: Golf: 18 holes at The Pointe at Lookout Mountain (Bill Johnston) and 18 holes at The Pointe on South Mountain (Forrest Richardson and Arthur Jack Snyder). Other amenities at Squaw Peak: eight lighted tennis courts, four indoor racquetball courts; stables; Sports Club with weight training, aerobics and exercise equipment; five heated swimming pools and spas. Tampatio Cliffs: 16 Plexipave tennis courts, indoor racquetball courts; stables, fitness room with steam and sauna; and six heated swimming pools. South Mountain: 10 Plexipave tennis courts and six indoor racquetball courts; stables; Sports Club with state-of-the-art exercise equipment, spa services, beauty salon and medical diagnostic testing; six heated swimming pools.

MEETING FACILITIES: Squaw Peak: more than 44,000 square feet of divisible meeting rooms. Tampatio Cliffs: more than 65,000 square feet of meeting and banquet facilities.

RATES: Single suites from $99; doubles from $109. Three-day, two-night golf, tennis and fitness packages from $180; two-day, one-night romance and relaxation packages from $120.

RESERVATIONS: Call (800) 876-4683.

Scottsdale Princess

An elegant tribute to Southwestern style

JUST 15 MINUTES NORTH OF Scottsdale, where the crowds and shops and traffic give way to Saguaro, cholla and barrel cactus, the Scottsdale Princess shimmers like a grand Spanish Colonial estate. Just when you think you've made a wrong turn in this vast expanse of desert, you've in fact entered a whole new world of elegance and comfort.

The Scottsdale Princess opened in December 1987 as the first U.S. resort of Princess Hotels International, and it set a standard that has proven difficult to duplicate. Its rather remote setting, a gorgeous 450 acres against the backdrop of the McDowell Mountains, accentuates a "get-away-from-it-all" allure. Despite its size—600 rooms, 11 restaurants and lounges, and an array of amenities—the resort exudes a serene, almost meditative mood. The hotel's terra cotta-colored walls, arches and collanades and Mexican barrel-tiled roof is a subtle celebration of classic Southwestern style. And if the hotel itself isn't enough to

draw city folks out into the heart of the Sonoran, there's another drawing card: great golf.

Adjacent to the Scottsdale Princess is a pair of 18-hole courses designed by the heralded team of Jay Morrish and former PGA Tour great Tom Weiskopf. Both courses are owned by the city of Scottsdale, thereby making them open to the public, and are managed by the PGA Tour. Of the two, the more heralded is the TPC of Scottsdale, which since 1987 has hosted the PGA Tour's Phoenix Open.

As a public facility designed to host a PGA Tour event, the TPC of Scottsdale presented a unique challenge to Morrish and Weiskopf. While moving an astonishing two million cubic yards of earth around the barren terrain, the designers had to come up with a layout that would prove challenging enough for the game's best players, yet one playable enough to be enjoyed (and played at a reasonable pace) by resort guests and weekend hackers. For the most part, they

succeeded. The course stretches to 7,038 yards and offers such tests as the 466-yard (and upwind) par-4 sixth and the 228-yard par-3 seventh. On the other hand, there's the 515-yard par-five 15th, which is reachable in two by virtually all professionals and most amateurs, but with an island green that heightens the risk considerably. There's also the tiny 303-yard, par-four 17th, which is eminently driveable for the tour's big hitters. But there's trouble here, too, in the form of a well-bun-kered green bordered to the left and rear by water.

While the Stadium Course is definitely worth a go while staying at the Scottsdale Princess, one may want to warm up on the 6,552-yard Desert Course, a more forgiving Morrish/Weiskopf design that emphasizes the target golf philosophy without as many hazards. It's also considerably

The TPC of Scottsdale is one of the few public facilities in the country to host a PGA Tour event.

easier on the wallet, with a peak season green fee of $16 compared to the Stadium's $75.

Back at the Scottsdale Princess, there's a plethora of post-golf indulgences. The truly active can serve up a couple of sets of tennis on the 10,000-seat stadium court that hosts the annual WCT Scottsdale Open, or get a workout and massage at the health and fitness center. The riding set can trot over to Horseworld, an adjacent 400-acre horse park with equestrian arenas, two polo fields (matches are played every Sunday, in season) and more than 480 permanent stables. And when evening rolls around, center stage at the Princess belongs to Marquesa.

There are several excellent restaurants within the confines of the Scottsdale Princess, but Marquesa is the resort's shining star. Having been honored for excellence by both *Esquire* and *USA Today*, Marquesa specializes in Catalan cuisine, an intermingling of dishes from Northeastern Spain, the French region of Sardinia and the Balearic Islands. This translates into a wonderful olive-oil based amalgamation of tomatoes, eggplant, seafood, beef, game, beans and pasta. Try the anec amb oporto (breast of duck sauteed with port wine and figs) followed by creme catalana (fresh berries and sweet creme with a burnt sugar glaze). Then retire to a graciously appointed guest room for a nightcap, perhaps by a roaring fire.

If it all sounds like something fit for royalty, so be it. In her first visit to the U.S., this Princess has left an indelible impression. ∎

Scottsdale Princess
Scottsdale, Arizona

LOCATION: 7575 East Princess Drive, Scottsdale, AZ 85255. North Scottsdale, approximately 20 minutes north of Phoenix Sky Harbor Airport.

ACCOMMODATIONS: 525 rooms, including 400 in the main building and 125 efficiency and one-bedroom casitas near the racquet club.

DINING/ENTERTAINMENT: Marquesa, gourmet dining in elegance for dinner only; Las Ventanas, informal bistro overlooking pool and golf courses; La Hacienda, traditional Mexican fare in authentic hacienda; Champions Bar & Grill, in the golf clubhouse for breakfast, lunch and dinner; Caballo Bayo, entertainment and dancing; Cazadores, piano music for cocktails and dancing; La Hacienda Bar and Lounge.

AMENITIES: Two 18-hole golf courses (Jay Morrish and Tom Weiskopf) including TPC Stadium Course that hosts the PGA Tour's Phoenix Open; 10 tennis courts (six lighted) including stadium court that hosts WCT-Scottsdale Open; three swimming pools; 10,000-square-foot health club and spa with racquetball and squash; Horseworld, 400-acre horse park adjacent to the property.

MEETING FACILITIES: 58,000 square feet of meeting space including 22,500-square-foot grand ballroom.

RATES: Standard rooms from $95; suites from $215. Golf, tennis, fitness and honeymoon packages from $118.

RESERVATIONS: Call (800) 255-0080 or (602) 585-4848.

Sheraton San Marcos

Where it all began

HAD IT NOT BEEN FOR A SLIGHTLY confused Spaniard and a progressive Phoenix veterinarian, the Sheraton San Marcos would simply be a mirage in the eastern Salt River Valley. And had it not been for the San Marcos, the "Valley of the Sun" may have never seen its first tourist.

It's true. Dr. Alexander Chandler's foresight in planning a resort in the Arizona desert in the early 1900s provided the Salt River Valley with an important national awareness and growth potential from the time statehood was first granted. Opened in 1913, the original San Marcos was the prototypical South-

western resort, which served for 66 years as a playground and retreat for heads of industry and celebrities from around the world. Clark Gable slept here, as did Joan Crawford, Bing Crosby, Erroll Flynn and Jimmy Stewart, and the ensuing publicity from these visits helped to encourage tourism to this ruggedly beautiful territory.

By the way, the aforementioned Spaniard was Friar Marcos de Niza, who made his way through the area in 1539 while searching for the Seven Cities of Cibola, mythical cities supposedly harboring gold and other treasures. While de Niza never struck it rich, he did get a resort named after him.

Today, the Sheraton San Marcos is situated on the downtown square in the appropriately named village of Chandler, just south of downtown Phoenix. Despite recent renovations to its guest rooms and conference facilities, the resort remains one of the finest examples of Mission Revival architecture in Arizona. Listed on the National Register of Historic Places, many of the hotel's original elements—most notably the trellised, vine-covered pergolas that surround the resort—remain intact.

The 18-hole golf course at San Marcos has quite a storied history itself. The course was originally layed out in

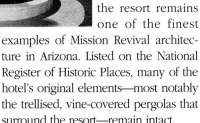

1913 by Harry Collis and Will Robinson, the husband of the hotel's first general manager. It was the first Arizona resort to offer its guests a golf course on the premises, and it was the state's first course to feature grass and water hazards. In 1928, Collis and William Watson of Los Angeles redesigned the course with a sprinkler system. Recently, the resort was the first in the country to introduce air-conditioned golf carts.

The par-72 golf course, which also has been recently renovated, is the quintessential resort layout: not terribly taxing (6,450 yards from the tips), with a liberal sprinkling of sand and water to keep things interesting. The resort also offers lighted tennis courts, two swimming pools, a weight room and

three fine restaurants including the European-flavored A.J.'s Cafe (named for Chandler) and the elegant 1912. San Marcos was honored by Sheraton corporate in 1988 for having the best food service in the chain's Western division. There's also 24-hour room service every day, a perk usually found only in resorts with higher star and diamond counts.

Also worth noting are the San Marcos meeting facilities, which account for a significant share of the resort's traffic. There's 26,000 square feet of space, including a 13-room conference center in the original San Marcos Hotel that can handle up to 700 participants.

The course at San Marcos was the first in Arizona to offer grass fairways and water hazards.

Banquet services has put together an interesting diversion called "Dinner in the Desert." Guests are transported by Jeep to the San Tan Mountain desert south of Chandler and, after a nature walk and some target shooting to stimulate the appetite, a dinner of steak and quail is served followed by a little Cotton-eyed Joe on the portable dance floor. Another version of "Dinner in the Desert" consists of a five-course gourmet meal with ballroom dancing under the stars. Formal dress is not required; guests are instead given tuxedo T-shirts to wear.

Who says innovation can't be fun? ■

SHERATON SAN MARCOS — CHANDLER, ARIZONA

LOCATION: One San Marcos Place, Chandler, AZ 85224; approximately 18 miles southeast of Phoenix Sky Harbor Airport.

ACCOMMODATIONS: 280 guest rooms and 17 suites.

DINING/ENTERTAINMENT: A.J.'s Cafe, informal, Europen-style cafe dining for breakfast, lunch, dinner and Sunday brunch; 1912, formal gourmet dining with Continental and regional fare for dinner only; Mulligan's Bar & Grill, informal dining at golf clubhouse for breakfast, lunch and cocktails; Cibola, a high-energy nightclub with disc jockey and dancing nightly.

AMENITIES: 18 holes of golf; four tennis courts; two swimming pools and whirlpool; fully equipped exercise/weight room; specialty and retail shops; adjacent Chandler Center for the Performing Arts.

MEETING FACILITIES: More than 26,000 square feet of divisible convention and banquet space, including a 13-room conference center, for groups of 20 to 700.

RATES: Standard rooms from $75; junior suites from $115; suites from $295.

RESERVATIONS: Call (800) 325-3535 or (602) 963-6655.

The Wigwam

Authentic Arizona at its finest

THE QUINTESSENTIAL DESERT RESORT, in one man's humble opinion, is one that effectively marries a great sense of tradition with a stellar array of amenities and services, cast against a backdrop of rugged desert terrain and majestic mountains rising into the cloudless sky.

In other words, The Wigwam Resort. It's downright painful to be objective about the retreat that helped establish Arizona as a tourist mecca in the 1930s, and which still pampers its guests in lavish luxury 60 years later. Fact is, The Wigwam offers all of the above and more. When speaking of great Arizona golf resorts—and you can wear out a lot of adjectives in such a discussion— this is as authentic as it gets.

Located 20 minutes west of Phoenix in Litchfield Park, The Wigwam is spread over a 75-acre oasis of stately palms, ornamental orange trees, lush lawns and flower gardens bursting with annuals. Its low-rise casitas, which house 241 guest rooms and suites, are nestled into the landscape and enveloped by the scent of surrounding bougainvilla and night-blooming jasmine.

Heading the list of amenities are three outstanding 18-hole golf courses, all of which give resort guests top priority for tee times. And the level of service is exemplary, part of the reason being that there are many second- and third-generation employees here.

Indeed, it's one big happy family at The Wigwam, and the patriarch is somewhat of a living legend in the hospitality industry. Cecil Ravenswood, a native Australian, is a veteran hotelier who has served at some of the world's finest facilities in New Zealand, Canada and the U.S. as well as his homeland. Having previously served as general manager at the nearby Arizona Biltmore, Ravenswood is no stranger to five-star/five-diamond quality. Neither is The Wigwam; the hotel has received Mobil and AAA's highest honors for several years running and is also a member of Preferred Hotels Worldwide, a marketing organization of 95 independently owned luxury hotels and resorts.

Like many of Arizona's other grand resorts, The Wigwam enjoys a rich and storied history. It began in 1915, when Paul Weeks Litchfield, the vice president and factory manager of Goodyear Tire & Rubber Company, developed a revolutionary new tire for the still-fledgling automobile. Problem was, the strong fabric required to make the tire could be woven only from staple cotton, which was grown only in the Georgia Sea Islands and the Nile Valley in Egypt. Boll weevils took care of the Sea Island crop, and German sub-

marines in World War I wreaked havoc on any shipments coming from Egypt. Litchfield needed a new North American source and he found it, albeit on a very limited scale, in southern Arizona, which approximated the Nile Valley's climactic conditions, irrigation and growth patterns. Defying the skeptics, Goodyear immediately purchased 16,000 acres along the Agua Fria River in 1916 and planted cotton seeds.

That first crop yielded 1,200 bales and, encouraged by its success, the company increased its holdings to 38,000 acres by 1921. Litchfield Park was subsequently founded as the hub of the empire with churches, schools and businesses, and by the winter of 1919, Organization House, the initial building of the present-day Wigwam Resort, was built to house and feed

company visitors. Guests were so enamored with the lodge, they fondly dubbed it "The Wigwam" and petitioned Goodyear to open the facilities to the public. On Thanksgiving Day 1929, The Wigwam was opened as a resort hotel with 13 guest rooms.

Goodyear retained ownership of The Wigwam until 1986, when it sold the resort to SunCor Development Company, a subsidiary of Arizona's Pinnacle West Capital Corporation. The new owners immediately began a $30-million refurbishment and restoration on the hotel and golf courses, reopening in October 1988 with its present configuration of 241 guest rooms. An additional $13-million expansion

Below: Guest casitas at The Wigwam are decorated in a decidedly Southwestern style.

was completed late last year, which added a 10,800-square-foot ballroom to the resort's conference facilities, as well as 90 new guest casitas.

It was money well spent, as the accommodations at The Wigwam are truly magnificent. Spacious and luxurious, guest rooms are decorated in the soft colors, textures and fabrics of the region, and appointed with such essentials as remote control TV, VCRs and honor bars. Should guests ever desire to leave such safe haven, the amenities include a magnificent pool area, nine lighted Plexipave tennis courts including a 500-seat stadium court, and riding stables. But perhaps more than anything else, The Wigwam is known for its golf.

Of the three courses at The Wigwam, the Robert Trent Jones-designed Gold Course has won the most accolades, and deservedly so. This is Jones Sr. at his diabolical best: 7,074 from the tips and a 74.9 rating, huge undulating greens and a multitude of water hazards and bunkers.

Tough? The 451-yard eighth hole is regarded as one of the most difficult par-fours in the state, and the par-five 10th stretches to a whopping 610 yards from the back tees (a mere 556 from the regular box). Thankfully, there are a variety of tee settings that make the course more palatable for players of lesser skill and/or nerve.

Jones also designed the Blue Course at The Wigwam. This is a good "starter" track that plays to just 5,960 yards and a par of 70, but it also features several water holes, numerous bunkers and large greens. The third course, West, was designed by the late Robert "Red" Lawrence, who penned several traditional courses throughout Arizona in the mid-1900s. At 6,865 yards, West is an equally stimulating test of golf and

THE WIGWAM — LITCHFIELD PARK, ARIZONA

LOCATION: West Indian School Road and Litchfield Park Road, Litchfield Park, AZ 85340; 23 miles from Sky Harbor Airport.

ACCOMMODATIONS: 241 rooms, 68 suites.

DINING/ENTERTAINMENT: The Terrace Dining Room, American cuisine, nightly dancing; The Grille on the Greens, steaks and seafood; The Arizona Kitchen, Southwestern theme; The Arizona Bar; The Pool Cabana; The Kachina Lounge, cocktails and afternoon tea.

AMENITIES: 54 holes of golf; nine lighted tennis courts; horseback riding; croquet; swimming; fitness and spa facilities; trap and skeet shooting; complimentary bicycles.

MEETING FACILITIES: Twenty-one meeting rooms accommodating 10 to 600.

RATES: From $80 to $355; golf packages from $109 to $356.

RESERVATIONS: Call (800) 327-0396.

visually appealing as well, winding around a meandering stream and five lakes.

Having satisfied one's recreational appetite, the focus can shift to those of a more gastronomical nature. Dining at The Wigwam comes under the auspices of chef Michael Garbin, a Brooklyn native who took Memphis by storm as executive chef of the Peabody Hotel (Chef of the Year in 1984) and also served at Denver's Brown Palace Hotel before coming to The Wigwam in 1988. Garbin holds court in three fine restaurants: The Terrace Dining Room, with fine American dining and dancing to Big Band sounds; The Grille on the Greens, offering grilled prime steaks and seafood; and The Arizona Kitchen, with a more casual Southwestern atmosphere with pizzas, meats, fish and game grilled over aromatic woods. And there is 24-hour room service for those who never want to leave their casita.

But for a little adventure, try touring the native desert on a breakfast horseback ride. Better yet, take a hayride to nearby Sunset Point for a evening steak broil and a spectacular Arizona sunset. You'll see what all the fuss is about at The Wigwam. As desert resorts go, it doesn't get much better than this. ■

Arizona Golf Resort

Unparalleled value for business or pleasure

IT'S ONE THING TO FIND TOP quality service and facilities in a golf resort. But when you can find quality and value at the same time, you've really got something. And when it comes to value, Arizona Golf Resort and Conference Center is a tough act to follow.

Located 30 minutes from Phoenix, Arizona Golf Resort is one of those rare destinations where a dollar goes much further than normal. Spread over 150 well-tended acres, accommodations comprise 162 rooms, suites and larger casitas. The standard rooms are comfortably appointed and come equipped with kitchenettes, while the suites and casitas are extremely spacious and offer full kitchens.

There's a variety of amenities on property including a very interesting 18-hole golf course. At first glance, this 6,574-yard, par-71 seems rather benign, with six par-threes and five par-fives. But out-of-bounds comes into play often, the greens are overly large and constantly inviting three putts, and four of the par-threes play more than 200 yards. But with five sets of tees, the course can be as playable or as challenging as one desires.

In addition to the standard golf packages, the resort also offers an "Overseeding Special," where they cut 50 percent off the regular package rate when the new grass is being planted. Nice touch.

Arizona Golf Resort offers a fine restaurant, Annabelle's, where the Prime Rib is renowned, and an adjacent lounge with entertainment. Its meeting facilities aren't grandiose, but with more than 10,000 square feet they easily accommodate smaller to medium-size groups.

In addition to its proximity to Scottsdale, the resort is within a well-struck 3-wood of three major shopping complexes: Superstition Springs Center, Fiesta Mall and the VF Factory Outlet Center. After all, guests of Arizona Golf Resort will have to do *something* with all that money they're saving. ∎

**Arizona Golf Resort
425 South Power Road
Mesa, AZ 85206**

LOCATION: East of Phoenix, approx. 30 minutes from Sky Harbor Airport.

ACCOMODATIONS: 162 deluxe rooms, fairway suites and lakeside casitas (one- and two-bedroom condominium suites available on request).

DINING/ENTERTAINMENT: Annabelle's, informal dining for breakfast, lunch, dinner and Sunday brunch, lounge offers live entertainment; Poolside Patio, dining and cocktails; 19th Green, light snacks and drinks overlooking golf course.

AMENITIES: 18 holes of golf; four tennis courts (two lighted); heated swimming pool; spas; bicycling; access to nearby health club (additional fee required).

MEETING FACILITIES: More than 10,000 square feet of meeting space including 4,048-square-foot combined ballroom and 2,500-square-foot outdoor patio courtyard.

RATES: Deluxe rooms from $59, lakeview executive suites from $69, and fairway suites & casitas from $99.

RESERVATIONS: Call (800) 528-8282 or (602) 832-3202.

Francisco Grande Resort & Golf Club

NESTLED IN THE CASA GRANDE Valley, some 45 miles south of Phoenix, Francisco Grande has long been known as a retreat for professional athletes. Horace Stoneham, the former owner of the San Francisco Giants, opened the resort in 1964 as the spring training home for his baseball team (hence the name "Francisco").

When the resort was sold and the Giants moved their camp to Phoenix in 1979, the California Angels used the facility until 1982. The USFL's Arizona Wranglers and Denver Gold also used the resort as their training headquarters in the early 1980s.

After extensive renovations and refurbishment in the mid-1980s, the "Grande" reopened to the public in 1987 with 112 guest rooms and suites, two very good restaurants, and an 18-hole golf course that offers outstanding bentgrass greens.

At 7,320 yards from the tips, the course is one of the longest in the state of Arizona. ■

**Francisco Grande Resort
26000 Gila Bend Highway
Casa Grande, AZ 85222**

LOCATION: 45 miles south of Phoenix.

ACCOMMODATIONS: 112 rooms and suites.

DINING/ENTERTAINMENT: The Palo Verde Room, fine dining for dinner; the Veranda, casual lunches and dinners; Franny Granny's Lounge, cocktails and entertainment.

AMENITIES: 18 holes of golf; three lighted tennis courts; swimming pool.

MEETING FACILITIES: 5,000 square feet of meeting and banquet space accommodating groups from five to 300.

RATES: Standard rooms from $49; suites from $89; packages from $67.50

RESERVATIONS: Call (602) 836-6444 or (800) 237-4238.

The Inn at McCormick Ranch

SITUATED ON THE SHORE OF Camelback Lake in the heart of Scottsdale, the intimate Inn at McCormick Ranch is a Valley of the Sun sleeper. What other Valley resort can offer sailing and windsurfing as amenities?

Yet what really sets the Inn apart is the ultra-friendly, highly personalized service, as well as its attractive array of accommodations. Guests choose from spacious Southwestern-flavored guest rooms with lakeside, garden or mountain views, or fully furnished two- and three-bedroom villas available by the day, week or month.

Indeed, staying a month at the Inn isn't unusual, especially if you're a golfer. The Inn not only offers guests preferential tee times at the Pine and Palm courses at McCormick Ranch Golf Club, but its golf packages also include play at five other area courses. And these are no dogtracks, either: the Arizona Biltmore; the Bob Cupp-designed Tatum Ranch Golf Club; Stonecreek Golf Club, one of the country's outstanding daily-fee facilities; Scottsdale Country Club; and Pete Dye's Karsten Golf Course at Arizona State University.

As for dining, many a dieter has been known to fall off the wagon over the chocolate taco at the Inn's highly regarded Pinon Grill.

Whether you're looking for peace and quiet, or all the activity you can ask for, the Inn at McCormick Ranch fills the bill in its own quiet, yet hospitable way. Surf's up! ■

Inn at McCormick Ranch
7401 N. Scottsdale Road
Scottsdale, AZ 85253

LOCATION: 25 minutes northeast of Phoenix Sky Harbor Airport.

ACCOMMODATIONS: 125 rooms, 50 villas.

DINING/ENTERTAINMENT: The Pinon Grill, Southwestern cuisine, breakfast, lunch, dinner; Diamondbacks Lounge, dancing and live entertainment.

AMENITIES: 36 holes of golf at McCormick Ranch Golf Club; tennis; outdoor swimming pool; Jacuzzi; private lake for sailing or canoeing.

MEETING FACILITIES: 5,000 square feet of flexible meeting space.

RATES: Standard hotel rooms from $49; suites from $140; villas from $150.

RESERVATIONS: Call (800) 243-1332.

Orange Tree Golf Resort

DESPITE OPENING JUST THREE YEARS ago, Scottsdale's Orange Tree Resort succeeds remarkably well at exuding the ambience and personal service of a long-standing country club. There's a good reason for that, however. Orange Tree was built around golf, not simply next to it.

Johnny Bulla designed the Orange Tree Golf Club nearly 40 years ago, and it's a mature, links design with 6,762 lush yards of beauty and challenge. As with many of the desert's more traditional courses, Orange Tree is relatively flat. But the challenge comes from the tree-lined fairways that are dotted with bunkers. There's a large lake that comes into play on the approach to holes nine and 18, but that's the extent of the water problems.

This course is just a flat-out joy to play, with three very reachable par-fives and some long, mean par-fours, particularly on the incoming side.

The club feel is carried over to the resort's other major amenity, a 25,000-square-foot racquet and fitness center with tennis and racquetball courts, weight rooms and a complete offering of health and beauty programs in its spa. A relatively small (14,000 square feet) conference facility is located in the main clubhouse.

The accommodations at Orange Tree are truly special; the staff's favorite analogy is that it's a 30-foot putt from one end of your suite to the other. There are 160 suites in all, with separate living and sleeping areas, two televisions and a VCR, a refrigerated wet bar with coffee maker, whirlpool baths and French doors leading to a private terrace.

It's almost as if you've never left home. Or your club, for that matter. ■

Orange Tree Golf Resort
10601 North 56th Street
Scottsdale, AZ 85254

LOCATION: 13 miles northeast of Phoenix.

ACCOMMODATIONS: 160 suites.

DINING/ENTERTAINMENT: Joe's Restaurant, American cuisine; The Fairway Pavilion, overlooking 18th green; The Cascades Cafe, poolside dining and beverages.

AMENITIES: 18 holes of golf; racquet and fitness club; aerobics center; health club with beauty salon.

MEETING FACILITIES: More than 14,000 square feet of meeting space.

RATES: Suites from $100.

RESERVATIONS: Call (800) 228-0386.

The Registry Resort

A hidden gem in the heart of the desert

IT DOESN'T SEEK THE NOTORIETY OF some of its bigger, brasher competitors in the Valley of the Sun, but The Registry Resort just seems to have a way of winning over its clientele. It's not difficult to understand why. A member of the "Leading Hotels of the World" fraternity, The Registry has a European flair in its intimacy, yet it is teeming with outstanding amenities, award-winning restaurants, and wonderfully cozy accommodations.

Golf at The Registry is paramount, with 36 holes at the McCormick Ranch Golf Club. Desmond Muirhead, whose sometimes radical designs have been both lauded and criticized in golf circles, is credited with both courses at McCormick Ranch—Palm and Pine—and both are as distinctive as their designer. Palm, playing to 7,021 yards from the tips, is immersed in water; it comes into play on 10 holes. Yet the most challenging carry of the wet stuff is presented merely as an option. The 398-yard, par-4 ninth hole offers two choices: a safer, but much longer inland route from tee to green, or the gambler's special, a drive to a peninsula landing area followed by an approach over water to a green flanked by four bunkers.

There is much less water on the Pine course (7,020 yards), but it comes into play at the most inopportune times. For instance, the excellent 422-yard, par-4 sixth features a lagoon that begins in the middle of the fairway approximately 185 yards from the green, and runs parallel down the left side to the green. Then there's the 451-yard, par-four 15th, a classic Muirhead design that requires a 170-yard carry over water off the tee, followed by another carry on the approach to an island green. No one ever accused Desmond of being boring.

If it's enough to make you take up tennis, The Registry offers a fine facility with 21 courts and a highly regarded instructional program. Further solace

can be found in the resort's 318 luxurious rooms, all of which offer touches normally found in five-star properties: twice-daily maid service, 24-hour room service, a complimentary newspaper each morning and same-day valet service. The resort also features one of the finest convention and banquet facilities in the Valley.

Dining at The Registry is a distinct pleasure. The fabulous Phoenician Room offers a sumptuous Sunday brunch, and Cafe Brioche provides a charming Country French atmosphere for its regional specialties. It's all done very elegantly, very tastefully, very European.

The Registry may not be the most recognized resort in the Phoenix/Scottsdale area, but there's certainly no secret to its allure. ■

**The Registry Resort
7171 North Scottsdale Road
Scottsdale, AZ 85253**

LOCATION: Twenty-five minutes northeast of Phoenix Sky Harbor Airport.

ACCOMMODATIONS: 318 guest rooms, villas and suites.

DINING/ENTERTAINMENT: La Champagne, classic Continental and American regional cuisine in award-winning surroundings; Cafe Brioche, casual breakfast, lunch and dinner in a country French setting; The Phoenician Room, spectacular showroom setting for Sunday brunch; Garden Patio, casual *al fresco* dining; Fountain Lounge; Poolside Bar and Kachina Lounge, cocktails and light snacks.

AMENITIES: 36 holes of golf at the McCormick Ranch Golf Club (Desmond Muirhead); 21 tennis courts; four swimming pools; spa; health and fitness center; jogging paths; children's programs (seasonal).

MEETING FACILITIES: More than 30,000 square feet of space including the 14,000-square-foot Crystal Ballroom.

RATES: Standard guest rooms from $95; villas and suites from $185. Golf and tennis packages available on request.

RESERVATIONS: Call (800) 247-9810 or (602) 991-3800.

Rio Verde Resort & Country Club

Privacy, beauty and great golf

FEW VACATION AND RESORT AREAS offer the seclusion, privacy and natural beauty of Rio Verde Resort & Country Club, an adult community of privately owned homes located 25 miles northeast of Scottsdale. Surrounded by the McDowell, Superstition and Mazatzal mountains and the Tonto National Forest, the lush Verde River Valley site is one of the state's most scenic areas.

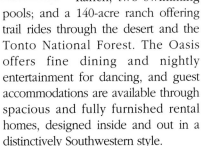

The land that encompasses Rio Verde has a history as colorful as the gold extracted from its neighboring mountains. Once a fertile homeland to the Hohokam Indians, the country club site occasionally surrenders bits of ancient pottery shards after a particularly heavy desert downpour. And evidence of the historic calvary outpost, Fort McDowell, has been found on the Rio Verde property as well.

Perhaps the main attraction at Rio Verde is its golf: 36 holes of beautiful, rolling fairways with outstanding mountain backdrops. Both the Quail Run course (6,547 yards) and the White Wing course (6,456 yards) are good tests of golf without being overly tricky. Homes border the fairways and greens of Quail Run, a well-bunkered track where water comes into play on eight holes including the par-five 18th, where the large green is surrounded on three sides by a lake and flanked by two large bunkers.

In addition to golf, there's a tennis program under the direction of Mike Davey, formerly of John Gardiner's Tennis Ranch; two swimming pools; and a 140-acre ranch offering trail rides through the desert and the Tonto National Forest. The Oasis offers fine dining and nightly entertainment for dancing, and guest accommodations are available through spacious and fully furnished rental homes, designed inside and out in a distinctively Southwestern style.

Despite its peaceful seclusion, Rio Verde is just minutes away from Scottsdale's business and cultural centers and 45 minutes from Phoenix Sky Harbor Airport. Close by, yet a world apart. ■

Rio Verde Resort & Country Club
Four Peaks Boulevard
Rio Verde, AZ 85255

LOCATION: 25 miles northeast of Scottsdale, 45 minutes from Phoenix Sky Harbor Airport.

ACCOMMODATIONS: Fully furnished rental homes ranging from two-bedroom, two baths (1,300 to 1,500 square feet) to two-bedroom plus den (2,000 to 2,500 square feet).

DINING/ENTERTAINMENT: The Oasis Restaurant and Lounge, dinner and dancing with live entertainment; weekly special events such as Western cook-outs.

AMENITIES: 36 holes of golf; six tennis courts (two lighted); two swimming pools; horseback riding; trout fishing at nearby Saguaro Lake.

MEETING FACILITIES: Private rooms at the Community Center for small gatherings and private parties.

RATES: Rental homes from $75 per night (three-night minimum) and $300 per week.

RESERVATIONS: Call (800) 233-7103.

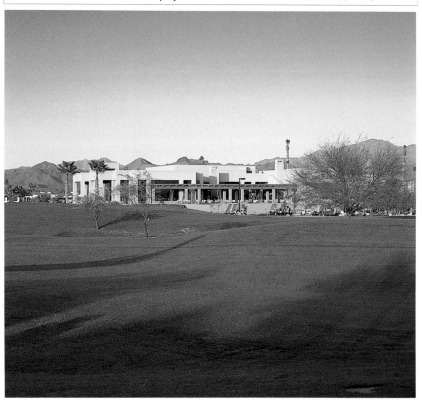

Places To Play

Valley of the Sun

Apache Junction/Queen Valley

Queen Valley Country Club
600 North Fairway Drive
Queen Valley, AZ 85219
(602) 463-2214
TYPE OF FACILITY: Semi-private Exec.
NO. OF HOLES: 18
DESIGN: Traditional
YARDAGE: 4,136-4,459
PAR: 66
PEAK RATES: $12 for nine, $20 for 18. Cart optional.

Roadhaven Golf Club
1000 S. Idaho Road
Apache Junction, AZ 85219
(602) 982-GOLF
TYPE OF FACILITY: Semi-private Exec.
NO. OF HOLES: Nine
DESIGN: Traditional
YARDAGE: 688-1,022
PAR: 27
PEAK RATES: $7 for nine, $14 for 18. Pull carts.

Carefree/Cave Creek

Eagle Creek Golf Club
5734 E. Rancho Manana Blvd.
Cave Creek, AZ 85331
(602) 252-3245
TYPE OF FACILITY: Semi-private
NO. OF HOLES: 18
DESIGN: Desert
YARDAGE: 5,011-6,400
PAR: 72
PEAK RATES: $55. Cart included.

Tatum Ranch Golf Club
4410 E. Dixiletta Drive
Cave Creek, AZ 85331
(602) 252-1230
TYPE OF FACILITY: Public
NO. OF HOLES: 18
DESIGN: Desert
YARDAGE: 5,609-6,870
PAR: 72
PEAK RATES: $65. Cart included.
COMMENTS: Bob Cupp design.

Chandler

Ocotillo Golf Club
3751 S. Clubhouse Drive
Chandler, AZ 85248
(602) 275-4355
TYPE OF FACILITY: Semi-private
NO. OF HOLES: 27
DESIGN: Traditional
YARDAGE: 5,124-6,729
PAR: Gold/Blue, 72; Gold/White,
71; Blue/White, 71.
PEAK RATES: $56. Cart included.

Sunbird Golf Resort
6250 Sunbird Blvd.
Chandler, AZ 85249
(602) 732-1955
TYPE OF FACILITY: Semi-private
Executive
NO. OF HOLES: 18
DESIGN: Desert
YARDAGE: 3,393-4,131
PAR: 65
PEAK RATES: $23. Cart optional.

El Mirage/Surprise

Happy Trails Golf Course
17200 W. Bell Road
Surprise, AZ 85374
(602) 975-5500
TYPE OF FACILITY: Public
NO. OF HOLES: 18
DESIGN: Links
YARDAGE: 5,146-6,652
PAR: 72
PEAK RATES: $25. Cart optional.

Pueblo El Mirage Country Club
11201 N. El Mirage Road
El Mirage, AZ 85335
(602) 583-0425
TYPE OF FACILITY: Semi-private
NO. OF HOLES: 18
DESIGN: Traditional
YARDAGE: 5,563-6,521
PAR: 72
PEAK RATES: $20. Cart optional.

Sun Village Golf Course
14300 W. Bell Road
Surprise, AZ 85374
(602) 584-5774
TYPE OF FACILITY: Semi-private
Executive

NO. OF HOLES: Nine
DESIGN: Traditional
YARDAGE: 759-1,029
PAR: 27
PEAK RATES: $5 for nine, $8 for 18.
Pull carts available.

Fountain Hills/Rio Verde

Fountain Hills Golf Club
10440 Indian Wells Drive
Fountain Hills, AZ 85268
(602) 837-1173
TYPE OF FACILITY: Semi-private

NO. OF HOLES: 18
DESIGN: Traditional
YARDAGE: 5,150-6,087
PAR: 71
PEAK RATES: $49.50. Cart included.

Glendale

Arrowhead Country Club
19888 N. 73rd Ave.
Glendale, AZ 85308
(602) 561-9625
TYPE OF FACILITY: Semi-private
NO. OF HOLES: 18
DESIGN: Desert
YARDAGE: 5,291-7,001
PAR: 72
PEAK RATES: $58. Cart included.

Bellair Golf Club
17233 N. 45th Ave.
Glendale, AZ 85308
(602) 978-0330
TYPE OF FACILITY: Public Executive
NO. OF HOLES: 18
DESIGN: Traditional
YARDAGE: 3,169-3,675
PAR: 59
PEAK RATES: $14. Cart optional.

Glen Lakes Golf Course
5450 W. Northern Ave.
Glendale, AZ 85301
(602) 939-7541
TYPE OF FACILITY: Public Executive
NO. OF HOLES: Nine
DESIGN: Traditional
YARDAGE: 2,195-2,381
PAR: 33
PEAK RATES: $11. Cart optional.

The Legend Golf Club
21025 N. 67th Ave.
Glendale, AZ 85308
(602) 561-9778
TYPE OF FACILITY: Public
NO. OF HOLES: 18
DESIGN: Traditional
YARDAGE: 5,286-6,977
PAR: 72
PEAK RATES: $42. Cart included.

Goodyear/Litchfield Park

Estrella Mountain Golf Course
South Bullard Road
Goodyear, AZ 85338
(602) 932-3714
TYPE OF FACILITY: Public

NO. OF HOLES: 18
DESIGN: Desert
YARDAGE: 5,720-6,415
PAR: 71
PEAK RATES: $16. Cart optional.

The Foothills Golf Club

Mesa

Apache Wells Country Club
5601 E. Hermosa Vista Dr.
Mesa, AZ 85205
(602) 830-4725
TYPE OF FACILITY: Semi-private
NO. OF HOLES: 18
DESIGN: Traditional
YARDAGE: 5,756-6,127
PAR: 71
PEAK RATES: $22. Cart optional.

Camelot Golf Club
6210 E. McKellips Road
Mesa, AZ 85205
(602) 832-0156
TYPE OF FACILITY: Public
NO. OF HOLES: 27
DESIGN: Traditional
YARDAGE: Championship, 4,658-5,600; Executive, 1,694-1,880.
PAR: Champ., 70; Exec., 31.
PEAK RATES: $25. Cart optional.

Desert Sands Golf Club
7400 E. Baseline Road
Mesa, AZ 85208
(602) 832-0210
TYPE OF FACILITY: Semi-private Exec.
NO. OF HOLES: 18
DESIGN: Traditional
YARDAGE: 3,900
PAR: 65
PEAK RATES: $14. Cart optional.

Dobson Ranch Golf Course
2155 S. Dobson Road
Mesa, AZ 85202
(602) 644-2291
TYPE OF FACILITY: Public
NO. OF HOLES: 18
DESIGN: Traditional
YARDAGE: 5,605-6,587
PAR: 72
PEAK RATES: $18. Cart optional.

Dreamland Villa Golf Club
5641 E. Albany
Mesa, AZ 85205
(602) 985-6591
TYPE OF FACILITY: Public Executive
NO. OF HOLES: Nine
DESIGN: Traditional
YARDAGE: 1,950
PAR: 31
PEAK RATES: $7.65. Cart optional.

Fiesta Lakes Golf Club
1415 S. Westwood Cir.
Mesa, AZ 85210
(602) 969-0377
TYPE OF FACILITY: Public Executive
NO. OF HOLES: Nine
DESIGN: Traditional
YARDAGE: 1,500
PAR: 29
PEAK RATES: $8. Pull carts.

Red Mountain Ranch Country Club
6425 E. Teton
Mesa, AZ 85205
(602) 985-0285
TYPE OF FACILITY: Semi-private
NO. OF HOLES: 18
DESIGN: Desert
YARDAGE: 4,982-6,977
PAR: 72
PEAK RATES: $79. Cart included.
COMMENTS: Very playable, dramatically scenic Pete Dye design.

Riverview Golf Course
2202 W. 8th Street
Mesa, AZ 85201
(602) 644-3515
TYPE OF FACILITY: Public
NO. OF HOLES: Nine
DESIGN: Traditional
YARDAGE: 2,600-3,150
PAR: 36
PEAK RATES: $10.50 for nine, $18 for 18. Cart optional.

Royal Palms Golf Club
1415 E. McKellips Road
Mesa, AZ 85203
(602) 964-1709
TYPE OF FACILITY: Public Executive
NO. OF HOLES: Nine
DESIGN: Traditional
YARDAGE: 1,350-1,501
PAR: 30
PEAK RATES: $7.50. Cart optional.

Sunland Village East Golf Course
2250 S. Buttercup
Mesa, AZ 85208
(602) 986-4079
TYPE OF FACILITY: Semi-private Exec.
NO. OF HOLES: 18
DESIGN: Traditional
YARDAGE: 3,296-3,689
PAR: 62
PEAK RATES: $8 for nine, $15.25 for 18. Cart optional.

Superstition Springs Golf Club
6542 E. Baseline
Mesa, AZ 85206
(602) 890-9009
TYPE OF FACILITY: Public
NO. OF HOLES: 18
DESIGN: Links

YARDAGE: 5,328-7,005
PAR: 72
PEAK RATES: $61. Cart included.
COMMENTS: Challenging and scenic public course. The 610-yard sixth is one of the most difficult par-fives in the state.

Superstition Springs

Sunland Village Golf Club
725 S. Rochester
Mesa, AZ 85206
(602) 832-3691
TYPE OF FACILITY: Semi-private Exec.
NO. OF HOLES: 18
DESIGN: Traditional
YARDAGE: 3,169-3,579
PAR: 62
PEAK RATES: $8.50 for nine, $15 for 18. Cart optional.

Viewpoint R.V. & Golf Resort
8700 E. University Drive
Mesa, AZ 85207
(602) 373-8715
TYPE OF FACILITY: Semi-private
NO. OF HOLES: Nine
DESIGN: Traditional
YARDAGE: 1,829-2,217
PAR: 34
PEAK RATES: $9 for nine, $15 for 18. Cart optional.

Paradise Valley

Stonecreek, The Golf Club
4435 E. Paradise Village Parkway South
Paradise Valley, AZ 85032
(602) 953-9110
TYPE OF FACILITY: Semi-private
NO. OF HOLES: 18
DESIGN: Links
YARDAGE: 5,098-6,839
PAR: 71
PEAK RATES: $71. Cart included.
COMMENTS: Magnificent facility that thrives on personal service. Worth the money.

Peoria

Country Meadows Golf Course
8411 N. 107th Avenue
Peoria, AZ 85345
(602) 972-1364
TYPE OF FACILITY: Semi-private Exec.
NO. OF HOLES: 18
DESIGN: Traditional
YARDAGE: 3,464-4,292
PAR: 63
PEAK RATES: $20. Cart optional.

The Vistas Club
18823 N. Country Club Parkway
Peoria, AZ 85382
(602) 566-1633
TYPE OF FACILITY: Public
NO. OF HOLES: 18
DESIGN: Traditional
YARDAGE: 5,223-6,493
PAR: 72
PEAK RATES: $24. Cart optional.

Westbrook Village Country Club
19260 N. Westbrook Parkway
Peoria, AZ 85345
(602) 933-0174
TYPE OF FACILITY: Semi-private

NO. OF HOLES: 18
DESIGN: Traditional
YARDAGE: 5,388-6,412
PAR: 71
PEAK RATES: $52. Cart included.

Phoenix

Ahwatukee Country Club
12432 S. 48th Street
Phoenix, AZ 85044
(602) 893-1161
TYPE OF FACILITY: Semi-private
NO. OF HOLES: 18
DESIGN: Traditional
YARDAGE: 5,506-6,698
PAR: 72
PEAK RATES: $30. Cart optional.

Ahwatukee Lakes Golf Course
13431 S. 44th Street
Phoenix, AZ 85044
(602) 893-3004
TYPE OF FACILITY: Public Executive
NO. OF HOLES: 18
DESIGN: Traditional
YARDAGE: 3,200-4,000
PAR: 60
PEAK RATES: $20. Cart optional.

Marriott's Mountain Shadows Golf Club

Cave Creek Golf Course
15202 N. 19th Ave.
Phoenix, AZ 85023
(602) 866-8076
TYPE OF FACILITY: Public
NO. OF HOLES: 18
DESIGN: Traditional
YARDAGE: 5,614-6,876
PAR: 72
PEAK RATES: $18. Cart optional.

El Caro Golf Club
2222 W. Royal Palm Road
Phoenix, AZ 85021
(602) 995-3664
TYPE OF FACILITY: Public Executive
NO. OF HOLES: 18
DESIGN: Traditional
YARDAGE: 3,021-3,330
PAR: 60
PEAK RATES: $15. Cart optional.

Encanto Golf Course
2705 N. 15th Avenue
Phoenix, AZ 85007
(602) 495-0333
TYPE OF FACILITY: Public
NO. OF HOLES: 18
DESIGN: Traditional
YARDAGE: 5,772-6,388
PAR: 70
PEAK RATES: $18. Cart optional.

Encanto Nine Golf Course
2300 N. 17th Avenue
Phoenix, AZ 85007
(602) 262-6870
TYPE OF FACILITY: Public Executive
NO. OF HOLES: Nine
DESIGN: Traditional
YARDAGE: 1,720
PAR: 30
PEAK RATES: $4.50. Cart optional.

The 500 Club at Adobe Dam
4707 Pinnacle Peak Road
Phoenix, AZ 85310
(602) 492-9500
TYPE OF FACILITY: Public
NO. OF HOLES: 18
DESIGN: Desert
YARDAGE: 5,600-6,700
PAR: 72
PEAK RATES: $22. Cart optional.

Maryvale Golf Course
5902 W. Indian School Road
Phoenix, AZ 85033
(602) 495-0444
TYPE OF FACILITY: Public
NO. OF HOLES: 18
DESIGN: Traditional
YARDAGE: 5,656-6,539
PAR: 72
PEAK RATES: $18. Cart optional.

Troon North

Tom Weiskopf's Foothills GC
2201 E. Clubhouse Drive
Phoenix, AZ 85044
(602) 460-8337
TYPE OF FACILITY: Public
NO. OF HOLES: 18
DESIGN: Desert

YARDAGE: 5,213-6,967
PAR: 72
PEAK RATES: $65. Cart included.
COMMENTS: Meticulously-groomed course designed by Weiskopf and partner Jay Morrish. Spectacular backdrops of Estrella Mountains.

Palo Verde Golf Course
6215 N. 15th Ave.
Phoenix, AZ 85015
(602) 249-9930
TYPE OF FACILITY: Public Executive
NO. OF HOLES: Nine
DESIGN: Traditional
YARDAGE: 1,820
PAR: 30
PEAK RATES: $6. Cart optional.

Papago Golf Course
5595 E. Moreland
Phoenix, AZ 85008
(602) 495-0555
TYPE OF FACILITY: Public
NO. OF HOLES: 18
DESIGN: Traditional
YARDAGE: 6,124-7,085
PAR: 72
PEAK RATES: $18. Cart optional.

Paradise Valley Park Golf Course
3505 E. Union Hills Drive
Phoenix, AZ 85032
(602) 992-7190
TYPE OF FACILITY: Public Executive
NO. OF HOLES: 18
DESIGN: Traditional
YARDAGE: 3,500-4,000
PAR: 61
PEAK RATES: $13. Cart optional.

Thunderbird Country Club
701 E. Thunderbird Trail
Phoenix, AZ 85040
(602) 243-1262
TYPE OF FACILITY: Public
NO. OF HOLES: 18
DESIGN: Links
YARDAGE: 6,054-6,459
PAR: 72
PEAK RATES: $35. Cart included.

The Valley Club Golf Course
5200 E. Camelback Road
Phoenix, AZ 85018
(602) 952-9313
TYPE OF FACILITY: Semi-private
NO. OF HOLES: Nine
DESIGN: Traditional
YARDAGE: 2,460
PAR: 36
PEAK RATES: $14. Cart optional.

Villa de Paz Golf Course
4220 N. 103rd Avenue
Phoenix, AZ 85039
(602) 877-1171
TYPE OF FACILITY: Public
NO. OF HOLES: 18
DESIGN: Traditional
YARDAGE: 5,288-6,140
PAR: 72
PEAK RATES: N/A. Cart optional.

Queen Creek

Apache Sun Golf Club
919 East Pima Road
Queen Creek, AZ 85242
(602) 987-9065
TYPE OF FACILITY: Public Executive
NO. OF HOLES: Nine
DESIGN: Traditional
YARDAGE: 2,329-2,661
PAR: 34
PEAK RATES: $10 for nine, $17 for
18. Cart optional.

Rancho Del Rey Golf Course
21515 Rancho Del Rey Blvd.
Queen Creek, AZ 85242
(602) 987-9059
TYPE OF FACILITY: Public
NO. OF HOLES: 18
DESIGN: Traditional
YARDAGE: 5,509-5,840
PAR: 71
PEAK RATES: $25. Cart included.

Scottsdale

Continental Golf Course
7920 E. Osborn Road
Scottsdale, AZ 85251
(602) 941-1585
TYPE OF FACILITY: Public Executive
NO. OF HOLES: 18
DESIGN: Traditional
YARDAGE: 3,381-3,766
PAR: 60
PEAK RATES: $29.50. Cart optional after 1 p.m.

Coronado Golf Club
2829 N. Miller Road
Scottsdale, AZ 85257
(602) 947-8364
TYPE OF FACILITY: Public Executive
NO. OF HOLES: Nine
DESIGN: Traditional
YARDAGE: 1,850-2,000
PAR: 31
PEAK RATES: $9. Cart optional.

Cypress Golf Course
10801 E. McDowell Road
Scottsdale, AZ 85256
(602) 946-5155
TYPE OF FACILITY: Public Executive
NO. OF HOLES: 18
DESIGN: Traditional
YARDAGE: Short nine, 1,700; Long nine, 2,480-3,466.
PAR: Short nine, 30; Long nine, 38.
PEAK RATES: Short nine, $6; Long nine, $9. Cart optional.

Mountain Shadows Golf Club
5641 E. Lincoln Drive
Scottsdale, AZ 85253
(602) 991-6656
TYPE OF FACILITY: Resort Executive
NO. OF HOLES: 18
DESIGN: Desert
YARDAGE: 2,595-3,060
PAR: 56
PEAK RATES: $42. Cart included.
COMMENTS: One of the West's finest Executive courses. Part of Marriott's Mountain Shadows Resort.

Pima Golf Resort
7331 N. Pima Road
Scottsdale, AZ 85258
(602) 948-3370
TYPE OF FACILITY: Public Resort
NO. OF HOLES: 18
DESIGN: Traditional
YARDAGE: 6,400-7,180
PAR: 72
PEAK RATES: $52. Cart included.
COMMENTS: Part of Ramada all-suites resort. Long course, with water in play on 10 holes. Great mountain views. Packages available.

The Karsten Course at ASU

Scottsdale Country Club
7702 E. Shea Blvd.
Scottsdale, AZ 85260
(602) 948-6911
Type of Facility: Resort Public
NO. OF HOLES: 27
DESIGN: Traditional
YARDAGE: 4,848-6,335
PAR: North/South, 70; North/East,
71; South/East, 71.
PEAK RATES: $60. Cart included.

Villa Monterey Golf Course
8100 E. Camelback Road
Scottsdale, AZ 85251
(602) 990-7100
TYPE OF FACILITY: Public Executive
NO. OF HOLES: Nine
DESIGN: Traditional
YARDAGE: 1,456-1,982
PAR: 31
PEAK RATES: $9. Cart optional.

Troon North
10320 E. Dynamite Blvd.
Scottsdale, AZ 85255
(602) 585-5300
TYPE OF FACILITY: Public Resort
NO. OF HOLES: 18
DESIGN: Desert
YARDAGE: 5,050-7,008
PAR: 72
PEAK RATE: $85. Cart included.
COMMENTS: Outstanding Tom

Weiskopf/Jay Morrish design, in
terms of beauty and playability.
Spectacular high Sonoran desert
landscape, winding through giant
saguaro, mequite, ocotillo, cholla,
and hundreds of topsy-turvy rock
formations. One of the desert's
best; well worth the time and
money. Master plan includes Four
Seasons hotel and 32,000-square-
foot clubhouse.

Sun City

Riverview Golf Course
16401 N. Del Webb Blvd.
Sun City, AZ 85351
(602) 876-3025
TYPE OF FACILITY: Semi-private

NO. OF HOLES: 18
DESIGN: Traditional
YARDAGE: 5,508-6,379
PAR: 72
PEAK RATES: $16. Carts optional.

Sun City West

Hillcrest Golf Club
20002 Star Ridge Drive
Sun City West, AZ 85375
(602) 584-1500
TYPE OF FACILITY: Semi-private
NO. OF HOLES: 18
DESIGN: Traditional
YARDAGE: 5,909-6,960
PAR: 72
PEAK RATES: $46. Cart included.

Trail Ridge Golf Course
21021 N. 151st Ave.
Sun City West, AZ 85375
(602) 546-0858
TYPE OF FACILITY: Semi-private
NO. OF HOLES: 18
DESIGN: Desert
YARDAGE: 5,522-6,605
PAR: 72
PEAK RATES: $18 for 18. Cart optional.

Tempe

Karsten Golf Course at ASU
1125 E. First Street
Tempe, AZ 85281
(602) 921-8070
TYPE OF FACILITY: Public
NO. OF HOLES: 18
DESIGN: Links
YARDAGE: 4,760-7,057
PAR: 72

PEAK RATES: $61. Cart included.
COMMENTS: Outstanding Pete Dye design on Arizona State University campus. Named in honor of Karsten Solheim, founder of Ping. Hosted 1992 Women's NCAA Championship. Tough finishing stretch, particularly 212-yard, par-three 16th and 471-yard, par-four 18th.

Troon North

Ken McDonald Golf Course
800 Divot Drive
Tempe, AZ 85283
(602) 350-5250
TYPE OF FACILITY: Public
NO. OF HOLES: 18
DESIGN: Traditional
YARDAGE: 5,872-6,743
PAR: 72
PEAK RATES: $14. Cart optional.

Pepperwood Golf Course
647 W. Baseline Road
Tempe, AZ 85283
(602) 831-9457
TYPE OF FACILITY: Public Executive
NO. OF HOLES: Nine
DESIGN: Traditional
YARDAGE: 1,685-2,010
PAR: 31
PEAK RATES: $8.50. Cart optional.

Rio Salado Golf Course
1490 E. Weber
Tempe, AZ 85281
(602) 990-1233
TYPE OF FACILITY: Public Executive
NO. OF HOLES: Nine
DESIGN: Traditional
YARDAGE: 2,167-2,600
PAR: 34
PEAK RATES: $9 for nine, $16.50 for 18, $7.50 for juniors. Cart optional.

Rolling Hills Golf Course
1415 N. Mill Avenue
Tempe, AZ 85281
(602) 350-5275
TYPE OF FACILITY: Public Executive
NO. OF HOLES: 18
DESIGN: Traditional
YARDAGE: North, 1,514-1,587; South, 1,782-2,230
PAR: North, 30; South, 32
PEAK RATES: $13. Cart optional.

The Karsten Course at ASU

Shalimar Golf Club
2032 E. Golf Avenue
Tempe, AZ 85282
(602) 838-0488
TYPE OF FACILITY: Public Executive

NO. OF HOLES: Nine
DESIGN: Traditional
YARDAGE: 1,859-2,400
PAR: 33
PEAK RATES: $9.50 for nine, $18 for 18.

Apache Junction/Queen Valley

Gold Canyon Golf Club
6100 S. Kings Ranch Road
Apache Junction, AZ 85219
(602) 982-9449
TYPE OF FACILITY: Semi-private Resort
NO. OF HOLES: 18
DESIGN: Desert

YARDAGE: 4,876-6,398
PAR: 71
PEAK RATES: $58. Cart included.
COMMENTS: Lush, well-maintained course set against Superstition Mountains. Part of intimate mountainside resort. Packages available.

Tucson

A city of 625,000, modern Tucson is a study of contrasts. Crumbling adobes are preserved among downtown highrises; resorts are nestled in rugged foothills where coyotes roam; cowboys (*real* working cowboys) rub shoulders with business executives; desert gullies are ofttimes drowned in monsoon-like storms; those who tire of soaking up rays at poolside hop in the car and, 30 minutes later, are schussing down a mountain.

It is perhaps the wild and exotic landscape that best characterizes the city. While lush Sonoran Desert vegetation rushes out in every direction, the mountains loom in the background against bright blue skies, which at night yield more visible stars in the center of town than most rural areas of the U.S. It is, inarguably, one of the most aesthetically refreshing areas of the U.S., and it's not surprising that the golf here is equally alluring. With superb courses designed by Jack Nicklaus and Tom Fazio, among others, there is a liberal mix of desert "target" golf courses and more traditional layouts.

Many of the local hotels and resorts offer special discounted rates throughout the year. It's an attractive package: great weather, breathtaking scenery, quality courses, affordable rates...and a touch of the exotic. If that fits your criteria for a great golf vacation, perhaps you should look no further.

Getting There

Tucson International, one of the fastest growing airports in the Southwest, is serviced by 14 domestic and international air carriers with more than 100 daily arrivals and departures. All major rental car companies are represented, and a number of ground transportation services are available to the downtown area. The city's major resorts offer round-trip limousine service at a nominal charge.

Weather

Winter temperatures in Tucson average highs of 65 degrees and lows of 38 degrees. Summer temperatures range from average highs of 98 degrees to lows of 70 degrees. Yet the year-round low humidity makes even the highest summer temperatures comfortable for golf, particularly if there's a breeze. The average yearly rainfall is just over 11 inches, most of which occurs in two rainy seasons: July through September and December through March. For maximum comfort on the golf course try scheduling your rounds in early morning or late afternoon in the summer (although some courses offer "suntan specials" for those hardy souls willing to compete against the noonday sun), and mid-day in the winter. When the sun begins to dip behind the mountains, the mercury falls rapidly.

Activities

While Tucson certainly doesn't lack for local color and attractions, there are some highly recommended excursions outside the city limits. Northeast of town on Sabino Canyon Road is Seven Falls, a 4 1/2-mile round-trip hike that provides the most camera-worthy scenery in the Tucson area. Shuttle service is also available. At the far east section of town is Agua Caliente Park, a former mineral hot springs retreat that is ideal for picnics. The 35-mile drive on the

narrow and winding Catalina Highway to Mt. Lemmon exposes five different climate and vegetation zones, from desert floor to Canadian air forest. Further out of town is the wonderful village of Tubac (45 miles south) with its collection of galleries and craft shops, and the Mexican border town of Nogales (65 miles south), an exhilarating change of pace that's great for shopping (be sure to negotiate the best price) and sightseeing.

Attractions

Perhaps the most famous attraction in Tucson, and one of its most beautiful, is Mission San Xavier Del Bac, the working mission founded in the early 1700s that serves as one of the country's finest examples of Spanish mission architecture. Among the city's many museums is the Flandreau Planetarium on the University of Arizona campus; the Pima Air Museum, featuring the third-largest collection of historic aircraft in the U.S.; the Arizona-Sonoran Desert Museum, featuring one of the finest zoos in the country; the Tucson Children's Musuem, located downtown in the historic Carnegie Library Building; and the Titan Missile Museum in nearby Green Valley, with tours of the abandoned missile complex. For a taste of the Old West it's hard to beat Old Tucson Studios, dubbed "Hollywood in the Desert" for the hundreds of movies and television shows filmed here since 1939. There's also Trail Dust Town east of Tucson, and 90 miles to the Southwest is Tombstone, the "town too tough to die," where Doc Holliday and Wyatt Earp hung out and the home of the O.K. Corral, Boot Hill and the Crystal Palace Saloon. Also south of town, toward Patagonia, are several ghost towns worthy of exploration.

Shopping

For the mall crowd there's the Tucson Mall (170 stores), Park Mall (120 stores) and El Con Mall (135 stores). On a smaller scale, Old Town Artisans in the El Presidio Historic District is an intimate marketplace for Arizona artisans as well as Native American and Latin American folk art, as is the Many Hands Courtyard, a Mexican village setting with handcrafted specialties and gifts. The Fourth Avenue Merchants

Association offers an historic shopping district of more than 100 stores and restaurants, and the Plaza Palomino offers a variety of specialty shops in a setting of tiled courtyards and fountains. Particular shops of note are The Bootery, with the largest selection of western footwear in town, and Corral Western Wear, which has sold authentic duds to both real and drugstore cowboys for 40 years.

Dining

For truly outstanding epicurean adventures try any (or all) of the following: Daniel's Restaurant and Trattoria, upscale Northern Italian with Art Deco decor; Cafe Terra Cotta, nouvelle southwestern fare, such as prawns stuffed with goat cheese and garlic custard in salsa vinaigrette with herbed hazelnuts; Janos, internationally acclaimed nouvelle cuisine; and The Tack Room, a Mobil Five-Star award winner since 1983 with Continental cuisine in an adobe hacienda setting. There's also Anthony's in the Catalinas, with excellent Continental cuisine, and Painted Desert, for nouvelle southwestern in a contemporary, artsy setting. A long-time Tucson favorite is Lil' Abner's Steakhouse, with mesquite-grilled steaks as well as ribs, chicken and a setting that will make you want to do the two-step. Don't forget your cowboy hat.

For More Information

The Metropolitan Tucson Convention and Visitors Bureau, 130 South Scott Avenue, Tucson, AZ 85701, (602) 624-1817.

Sheraton El Conquistador

The pioneer of Tucson continues to blaze trails

THEY CAME. THEY SAW. THEY GAMBLED. This is not about motorcoach travellers in Las Vegas. It's a somewhat more conservative lot known collectively as the Sheraton Corporation. It was 1982, and the hospitality conglomerate had swept into Southern Arizona seeking a site for its next resort complex. The chosen location was, at the time, anything but conventional: a rugged but dramatically scenic 150-acre tract in the Upper Sonoran Desert, set along the cliffs of Pusch Ridge in the Santa Catalina Mountains and adjacent to the Coronado National Forest. For Sheraton, success wasn't just a matter of having vacationers and meeting planners "discover" Tucson. The key was getting them to come 10 more miles into the high country.

The gamble paid off. As increasing numbers of people came to Tucson, so did they discover the Sheraton El Conquistador. Today, the "Old Pueblo," as it is affectionately known, is a lauded, self-contained destination with more holes of golf (45) than any other resort in this part of the state, an outstanding array of restaurants and other amenities, and an attractive selection of rooms and suites. Bolstered by the addition of the former Canada Hills Country Club in 1989, the El Conquistador has become the high desert's most prolific success story.

Golf at El Conquistador consists of a nine-hole course, perhaps the finest track of its kind in the country, surrounding the 440-room hotel, as well as 36 holes spread out among the El Conquistador Country Club, the former Canada Hills property located three miles from the resort. Being in the high desert foothills, the courses are designed for mountain-style play with deceptive changes in elevation. Gullies, ravines, natural sand washes and cacti complement the man-made hazards built into the courses.

The resort course sits at the base of Pusch Ridge in lushly vegetated desert terrain dotted with giant saguaro, ocotillo and cholla cacti. Although playing to just 2,759 yards from the tips, this is no tip-toe through the tumbleweeds. There are elevation changes up to 175 feet throughout the course. The par-fours range from 421 yards (No. 1) to 284 yards (No. 2); par-threes range from 191 (No. 4) to 111 (No. 7). It's the

course that the El Conquistador golf staff plays on their days off, if that tells you anything. If that doesn't tell you anything, maybe this will: The course record for the par-34 is a miserly 32.

Over at the El Conquistador Country Club, the aptly named Sunrise and Sunset courses offer tight, rolling fairways and large, multi-tiered greens with clustered bunkering and stands of mesquite and palo verde. Sunrise plays to 6,715 yards and features one of the finest par-threes in Tucson, the 188-yard eighth. Because the tee is elevated, the wind often plays havoc with shots to the two-tiered and well bunkered green, narrow and deep, that drops off some 30 feet into the desert. The feature hole on the 6,763-yard Sunset Course is its hardest, the 555-yard, par-5 fifth, where the approach must carry a small pond to an elevated green bulkheaded by large boulders.

Adhering to the philosophy that great golf and breathtaking scenery aren't the only things that draw people to this little corner of heaven, the El Conquistador is also one of Tucson's finest resorts for racquet sports. Between the hotel and the country club, there are 31 lighted tennis courts, including a 1,200-seat stadium and 12 indoor racquetball courts. The dining options are distinctive and delightful; most notably, the elegant La Vista at the country club, and the magnificent

Affectionately known as Old Pueblo, the Sheraton El Conquistador offers more holes of golf (45) than any other resort in the Upper Sonoran Desert.

THE AMERICAN SOUTHWEST

White Dove at the hotel, where I highly recommend a main course of fresh coho "burro de orro," (don't panic, "burro" has nothing to do with the actual content). And one of the El Conquistador's original calling cards (the convention center encompassing nearly 32,000 square feet of space) still brings them out to the desert in droves. A $5-million renovation completed in 1988 put a little shine on the apple, so to speak. El Conquistador continues to garner national kudos, being a perennial member of the Four Star/Four Diamond list, as well as a Gold Key recipient from *Meeting and Conven-*

tions magazine for six consecutive years.

The word's out; no reason to hedge bets anymore. What once was a gamble is now a sure thing. ∎

SHERATON EL CONQUISTADOR — TUCSON, ARIZ.

LOCATION: 10000 North Oracle Road, Tucson, AZ 85737; 10 miles northwest of Tucson International Airport.

ACCOMMODATIONS: 440 guest rooms including 100 casita units and suites.

DINING/ENTERTAINMENT: The Sundance Cafe, casual dining; The White Dove, Continental and Southwestern cuisine in elegant setting; The Last Territory, steaks and country music; Dos Locos Cantina, authentic Mexican fare and mariachi music, dancing nightly; La Vista, gourmet dining and spectacular views at El Conquistador Country Club.

AMENITIES: 45 holes of golf (nine at Sheraton El Conquistador Resort and 36 at nearby El Conquistador Country Club; 31 lighted tennis courts; 12 racquetball courts; fitness center; two swimming pools; Jacuzzis; horseback riding.

MEETING FACILITIES: More than 31,000 square feet of conference space, including an 11,900-square-foot ballroom and 14 breakout rooms.

RATES: Standard rooms from $90; junior suites from $115; casita suites from $125.

RESERVATIONS: Call (800) 325-7832 or (602) 742-7000.

Tucson National

Legendary appeal takes a new direction

IT'S GOT A NEW NAME, NEW OWNERS and a new attitude. But the tradition of excellence that has made Tucson National Golf & Conference Resort the granddaddy of this city's resort properties is as firmly entrenched as ever.

Purchased in January 1990 by First Interstate Bank, Tucson National received a welcome infusion of more than $1.5 million for improving the resort facility and its 27-hole golf course, as well as training the staff on the importance of guest service. The timing couldn't have been better; the National was losing guests to its newer and larger competitors, and it had already lost the PGA Tour's Northern Telecom Tucson Open, which severed a 15-year relationship with the resort in 1981. Having won Mobil's Four-Star designation since its opening in 1962, the resort was nevertheless ready for a facelift.

Enter First Interstate. One of the first orders of business was changing the resort's name from Tucson National Resort & Spa. The new name, according to new general manager Charles Dyke, accentuated the resort's major selling points—its championship-caliber course and an equally impressive, albeit small, corporate meeting facility. Once the commitment was made for the golf course renovations, Dyke negotiated the return of the Tucson Open, which had split time between the city's public Randolph Park course and the TPC at StarPass. The tournament returned in 1992, with the National hosting half of the first two rounds and all of the final 36 holes.

Perhaps the most alluring aspect of the original 18 holes at Tucson National is that they bear no resemblance whatsoever to "desert" golf. Designed in 1960 by Robert Bruce Harris and later refined by Bruce Devlin and Bob von Hagge, the course wasn't subjected to the same land and water restrictions placed on modern-day courses. Thus, you'll experience the Orange and Gold nines in peak form: lush, wide-open fairways with a traditional routing, Bermuda tees and fairways, and bentgrass greens.

The Orange/Gold championship rota plays 7,108 yards and offers some excellent tests of golf mettle. Perhaps most noteworthy are the finishing holes. Orange No. 9 is a par-four of 438 yards that gently doglegs right around a lake to a sharply elevated green, sloping steeply from back to front and surrounded by bunkers. The Gold ninth is a 439-yard par-four that plays straightaway, but uphill and into the prevailing wind to a large, sloping green.

The Green nine, the newest of the three, is more of a desert design, with much of the natural terrain in play. It's much shorter than its counterparts, just 3,222 yards from the tips, with just one par-four playing longer than 400 yards and the longest par-three stretching just 168 yards. Like its sister courses, however, it is consistently immaculate in conditioning, and a great warm-up for a bout with the tournament track.

The meeting facilities at Tucson National total just 15,000 square feet—miniscule by most resorts' gargantuan standards—but its track record speaks for itself. National enjoys a phenomenal return ratio among its small and midsized clients, with two divisible ballrooms, nine meeting rooms and additional outdoor space that can expand the facilities to 30,000 square feet. Golf is a great hook for National's group business, as is the resort's 167 guest suites, many of which have fireplaces, kitchens and other extras. The guest rooms also benefitted from the resort's refurbishing, as did National's main kitchen facility, which services the resort's main dining room, two lounges and room service.

The only facet of Tucson National

The wide-open design at Tucson National is a welcome change of pace from desert target golf.

that seemingly got lost in the shuffle was its magnificent spa. Not to worry; its reputation precedes it, which more than makes up for being dropped from the resort's original name. Few European spas can surpass, or even match, the variety of services and amenities here.

After the requisite massage and loofah scrub, men will want to try the Russian Bath, a special steam room that opens pores and reduces toxicity in the system. The ladies, meanwhile, may opt for the panthermal, which breaks down cells that form cellulite. Whatever the choice, guests are guaranteed to emerge revitalized.

Indeed, revitalization is the buzz word around the resort these days. Tucson National appears to be back and better than ever, and that's not exactly good news for the competition. ■

TUCSON NATIONAL — TUCSON, ARIZONA

LOCATION: 2727 West Club Drive, Tucson, AZ 85741; 30 minutes from Tucson International Airport.

ACCOMMODATIONS: 170 villa suites.

DINING/ENTERTAINMENT: The Fiesta Room, American cuisine in a semi-formal setting for breakfast, lunch and dinner; The Fiesta Bar, cocktail service adjacent to the main dining room; the Bella Vista Lounge, cocktail service with piano entertainment on weekends.

AMENITIES: 27 holes of golf (Robert Bruce Harris, Bruce Devlin/Bob von Hagge); 14,000-square-foot spa with an array of health and fitness programs and services.

MEETING FACILITIES: 15,000 square feet including two divisible ballrooms and nine conference rooms.

RATES: Villa suites from $75

RESERVATIONS: Call (602) 297-2271.

Ventana Canyon

Created by nature, enhanced by man

JUST NORTH OF TUCSON, AS THE Catalina Mountains rise before you, the first vestiges of Ventana Canyon appear. Subtly graceful, yet impossible to ignore, Ventana is a development of superlatives. Nestled at the base of Tucson's most imposing mountain range, and rich with the flavor of the Sonoran Desert, Ventana (Spanish for "window") is one of the most stunning marriages of man and nature ever accomplished.

Ventana Canyon consists of Loews Ventana Canyon Resort and the Ventana Canyon Golf & Racquet Club. These two very distinctive yet equally magnificent properties are tied together by two men: Bill Estes, the developer who took a chance on remodeling an uninhabited edge of a desert hillside, and Tom Fazio, who created the two excellent golf courses that adjoin the development Estes created.

Loews is part of a 1,050-acre development created by Estes and Catalina Properties, Inc. It was a project so environmentally aware that, during the early stages of development, the entire project was shifted for the sake of one 300-year-old saguaro cactus.

Vividly set into the hillside, the private patios of the hotel's 400 guest rooms and suites suggest the cliff dwellings that were so much a part of early settlements in Tucson. Around the grounds, secluded paths and terraces wind through virgin groves of mesquite, squawbush and blue paloverde.

Inside the hotel, it's definitely 21st century charm and elegance. Original juried pieces by Arizona artists are displayed throughout. The hotel's signature restaurant, the Ventana Room, offers five-star French cuisine in a romantic setting, complete with harpist and a sensational view of the city lights of Tucson. The spacious guest rooms and suites are decidedly Southwestern in decor, and feature oversized marble baths, three telephones and private balconies overlooking a man-made waterfall behind the 18th green of the Canyon golf course.

Opened in 1989, the Canyon Course is a tantalizing target track that was named one of the country's best new resort courses that year. Brimming with roadrunners, jackrabbits and an occasional coyote, the front nine of Canyon cuts through the visually stunning Esperero Canyon to the difficult ninth hole, a 416-yard par-four that plays uphill to a well-bunkered, partially hidden green. The back nine of Canyon is highlighted by the beautiful par-three 13th, which plays 159 yards downhill and offers views of up to 100 miles south to the Mexican border. There's also the 503-yard, par-five 18th, a slight-

ly uphill test that is reachable in two shots, but with a green that is protected by a natural wash in front and water to the right and rear.

Just down the hillside, through a maze of hundreds of saguaro cacti, lies the Ventana Canyon Golf & Racquet Club, a facility created to entertain those who joined the private club or who were visiting the property with an eye toward buying homesites along the golf course or on the mountainside. The club is open to the public for limited bookings, however, and in terms of setting and room quality, it ranks as one of the finest intimate hotels in the country. Its 48 luxury suites range from

800 to 1,500 square feet with full kitchens, dining areas, large baths with oversized tubs, living rooms and magnificent views from private balconies or patios.

The Club also features 12 lighted tennis courts, a 25-meter pool, meeting facilities, an exercise area, a fine dining room, lounges and access to the Mountain Course, a Fazio gem that has been rated not only as the best course in Tucson but as the finest resort course in the state.

Fazio admits that the Mountain

Guest rooms at Loews Ventana Canyon Resort offer sweeping views of the Canyon Course's 18th green.

Course was one of the most difficult projects he has faced because the site offered nothing but rock and native vegetation, and the developers were totally committed to the preservation of the natural habitat. The result is a desert masterpiece, carved from the mountainside and the scraggy Sonoran floor with impeccable precision. With tees ranging from 4,780 yards (and a 67.8 rating) to 6,969 yards (74.1), it's also a damn good course.

The most famous hole on the golf course, and probably the most expensive hole Fazio has ever built, is the "hole-in-the-wall" par-3 third. Playing much shorter than the 107 yards from the tips, it calls for a tee shot from atop rock outcroppings over a deep canyon of cacti to a severely undulating green set cliffside. Put it on this green and it'll make your vacation...but par is still no guarantee. The back of the two-tiered green rises sharply uphill, and when the pin is back it takes consummate skill to get down in two.

With the area virtually inaccessible by trucks, Fazio's crew had to take rocks and dirt out by hand on pulley systems—on tripods by bucket—like an old mining operation. The cost for this one absolutely picturesque hole: close to $600,000.

"Both the Canyon and Mountain courses are outstanding examples of my principles of design," says Fazio. "A course should be visually strong, environmentally sensitive and relative, dramatic, flowing and have style."

Style, indeed. That's something that will never run short at Ventana Canyon. ■

Loews Ventana Canyon Resort Ventana Canyon Golf & Racquet Club

LOCATION: Resort: 7000 North Resort Drive, Tucson, AZ 85715. Golf & Racquet Club: 6200 North Clubhouse Lane, Tucson, AZ 85715. Fourteen miles north of Tucson International Airport.

ACCOMMODATIONS: Resort: 400 rooms and suites. Ventana Canyon Golf & Racquet Club: 48 one- and two-bedroom club suites.

DINING/ENTERTAINMENT: Resort: The Ventana Room; Canyon Cafe; Bill's Grill; Flying V Bar & Grill. Golf & Racquet Club: Clubhouse Dining Room; Terrace Lounge; Fireside Lounge.

AMENITIES: Resort: 18-hole Canyon Course (Tom Fazio); Spa & Tennis Club with 10 courts, exercise equipment, aerobics, sauna, lap and therapy pools; croquet lawn; fitness trail. Golf & Racquet Club: 18-hole Mountain Course (Tom Fazio); 12 tennis courts; pool; men's and women's spas; exercise room.

MEETING FACILITIES: Resort: 37,000 square feet of meeting and exhibit space accommodating up to 1,200. Golf & Racquet Club: 2,000 square feet in two meeting/banquet rooms.

RATES: Resort: Standard rooms from $95; suites from $135; golf, tennis, fitness and romance packages available from $245. Golf & Racquet Club: one-bedroom suites from $90; two-bedroom suites from $185.

RESERVATIONS: Loews Ventana Canyon Resort: (800) 234-5117 or (602) 299-2020. Ventana Canyon Golf & Racquet Club: (800) 828-5701 or (602) 577-1400.

Westin La Paloma

Building success from the ground up

MENTION LA PALOMA TO THE seasoned Southwestern traveler, and the name-dropping will begin: Westin, Nicklaus, Seaver, Rogers, Gladwin & Harmony...

Well, maybe some aren't as recognizable as others. Yet while Westin boasts ownership of this magnificent $100-million resort, and Jack Nicklaus provides the property's 27 holes of golf instant credibility, it's these other, lesser-known folk who deserve much of the credit for creating a destination that's superbly sensitive to the Sonoran desert surroundings.

It was the initial goal of Douglas Seaver & Associates, the architectural firm charged with designing the Westin La Paloma, to heed special sensitivity to the land, to enhance and not detract. It was the early '80s, and environmentalists and long-time Tucson residents were intent on monitoring the impact of development on its surroundings. In order to secure the necessary zoning variance to build the resort, the developers had to agree to preserve the vast saguaro cactus population on the 709-acre property, some of which were more than 150 years old. It thus be-

came the task of Rogers, Gladwin & Harmony, landscape architects and planners, to determine how many saguaros were in existence and then plan the transplant process.

The arduous task required aerial surveys, in which the mature saguaros were identified by the shadows they cast in the photographs. Of the 8,056 saguaros ultimately counted, 7,224 were saved, with more than 1,000 being physically transferred to temporary holding facilities during construction of the resort. Additionally, the firm oversaw the transplanting of 15,000 other species of cacti, as well as 50 mesquite trees. The execution of this monumental task earned Rogers, Gladwin & Harmony extensive national recognition, and in 1984 the firm received a special Award of Merit from the American Society of Landscape Architects.

Re-enter Douglas Seaver & Associates, who created the 487-room Westin La Paloma as a village of 27 separate buildings. The hotel's Southwest Mission Revival architecture complements its Sonoran surroundings, and its signature color, La Paloma Rose, plays off

the dusty rose hue in the desert sunset. The theme is continued in each of the guest rooms, with Southwestern-flavored furnishings and appointments such as separate makeup areas outside the baths, armoirs with concealed remote-control television, oversized closets, large sitting room areas and private exterior entrances.

The amenity base at La Paloma is outstanding (tennis, racquetball, swimming, health club, etc.), and no one will want for refreshment with nine restaurants and lounges and 24-hour room service from which to choose. There is conference space equipped to handle more than 2,000. But the primary diversion at La Paloma bears the signature of a critter rarely found in these parts. In fact, La Paloma is the Golden Bear's only true resort course in Arizona.

The three immaculately conditioned nines at La Paloma—Hill, Ridge and Canyon—represent desert target golf at

its finest, no surprise since Nicklaus virtually invented the concept at Scottsdale's private Desert Highlands development. The Ridge/Canyon rota is the sternest test at 7,088 yards and a 142 slope rating; the easiest that it gets is 6,997 and 135 (Hill and Canyon). Still, there are as many as five sets of tees on some holes, and forecaddies accompany each foursome to keep you out of as much trouble as possible.

The strongest holes are Ridge No. 4, a 199-yard par-three playing over the edge of a canyon with the Santa Catalina Mountains in the background; Canyon No. 7, a 445-yard par-four that sharply doglegs left with a blind approach to a green cut into a hillside 30 feet above the fairway; and Hill No. 5, a massive 465-yard par-four where the approach is through a long valley that

Designed by Jack Nicklaus, the 27 holes at La Paloma represent desert 'target golf' at its finest.

opens up behind the green with panoramic views of Tucson.

Here's a hint: warm up to desert strategy by playing Hill first. And reserve a few extra days for your stay at La Paloma. You'll come away with both a new-found appreciation for environmental preservation and the people—famous and otherwise—who made it all happen. ■

WESTIN LA PALOMA — TUCSON, ARIZONA

LOCATION: 3800 E. Sunrise Drive, Tucson, AZ 85718; 10 miles north of the business district, 17 miles north of downtown.

ACCOMMODATIONS: 487 guest rooms including 41 suites.

DINING/ENTERTAINMENT: Desert Garden, all-day dining and Sunday brunch; La Paloma Dining Room, American cuisine, jackets required; La Villa, fine dining in Southwestern hacienda; Sabinos, swim-up service poolside; Courtside Deli, sandwiches and salads at Tennis Club; Desert Garden Lounge, cocktails and evening entertainment; Cactus Club, sports bar; 19th Hole.

AMENITIES: 27 holes of golf (Jack Nicklaus); 12 tennis courts; swimming pool with waterslide and swim-up bar; health club with Nautilus, racquetball and aerobics; Personal Services Center, massages, facials, etc.; jogging.

MEETING FACILITIES: 42,000 square feet in main building, including 18,000-square-foot ballroom; hospitality suites, two boardrooms.

RATES: Deluxe rooms from $140; Royal Oasis Club rooms from $240; suites from $195. Golf, tennis and other packages available.

RESERVATIONS: Call (800) 876-3683 or (602) 742-6000.

Hidden Gems

Rio Rico Resort & Country Club

The best-kept secret in the Valley

NESTLED IN THE SANTA CRUZ RIVER Valley just a few miles north of the Mexican border town of Nogales lies one of Arizona's best kept secrets. Rio Rico Resort & Country Club rises 4,000 feet amidst the Cayetano Mountain range, offering a delightful year-round climate rarely enjoyed in southern Arizona.

Close proximity to Nogales, as well as countless other colorful border towns, opens up a world of shopping, dining and entertainment opportunities. The Rio Rico hotel has recently undergone a major renovation and refurbishment under the direction of veteran hotelier Misharo "Mike" Ykemiyashiro.

Best of all is Rio Rico's golf course, designed by Robert Trent Jones Sr. A classic layout that ranges from 5,577 to 7,119 yards, the course features a sweeping, open front nine that runs along the river with magnificent mountain vistas.

Rio Rico offers tremendous value as well, with some excellent golf packages offered from May through September when most golfers are fleeing the Valley of the Sun for higher ground.

In fact, one has to wonder just how Trent Jones found this place to begin with. But he did, and we can all thank him by simply keeping the secret to ourselves. ∎

Rio Rico Resort & Country Club
1550 Camino a la Posada
Rio Rico, AZ 85621

LOCATION: 45 minutes south of Tucson, 12 miles north of the Mexican border.

ACCOMMODATIONS: 160 guest rooms; 10 one-bedroom suites; five two-bedroom apartments.

DINING/ENTERTAINMENT: La Cima, regional and American cuisine for breakfast, lunch, dinner; Cantina Lounge, cocktails, live entertainment.

AMENITIES: 18 holes of golf (Robert Trent Jones Sr.), horseback riding, hiking, swimming, Jacuzzi.

MEETING FACILITIES: More than 10,400 square feet accommodating 10 to 600.

RATES: Standard rooms from $70; suites from $145; apartments from $195. Three-day golf packages available from $121.

RESERVATIONS: Call (800) 288-4746 or (602) 281-1901.

Tubac Golf Resort

An historic ranch rekindles a great golf tradition

TO MY KNOWLEDGE, HOPE AND Crosby never did a road picture in Tubac, Arizona's oldest settlement in the Santa Cruz River Valley, some 40 miles south of Tucson. But Bing found his way here with some golfing buddies, and what resulted is Tubac Golf Resort.

This is a place for those who truly want to get away from it all on a golf vacation. If you can take the rural environs, just a few miles from the Mexican border, you'll be in for a real treat. Thanks to a very sensitive restoration effort in 1990, modern amenities are blended with the historic character of the site to offer one of Arizona's most unique destinations.

Tubac Golf Resort, known as Otero Ranch to the locals, is situated between the Santa Rita and Tumacacori mountains in the Santa Cruz River Valley, with abundant desert vegetation and an elevation of 3,500 feet. Generations of the Otero family lived on the site from the 1700s to 1958, when Crosby and a group of investors bought the ranch and turned it into Tubac Valley Country Club. Naturally, a golf course was part of the picture (Red Lawrence designed it), as were 32 guest rooms. The family

ranch house became a recreation center; today, it serves as the resort's meeting facilities. The stables were converted to an excellent restaurant, The Montura, with adobe walls, Mexican and Native American glassware and pottery and some of the finest regional cuisine in this part of the country.

The golf course is a scenic track, rolling through stands of cottonwood and mesquite against a picturesque mountain backdrop. Length (6,957 yards) isn't the only challenge here. The Santa Cruz River bisects the property and must be carried at the 305-yard, par-four 13th and the 413-yard, par-four 18th. It also comes into play from tee to green at the brutish 575-yard, par-five 16th.

Accommodations are spaciously comfortable one- and two-room units, some with kitchens and all with wood-burning fireplaces that maintain the resort's family ranch ambience. There are numerous trails for hiking and horseback riding, yet the resort's convenient location and interstate access make it easy for guests to venture out to discover the many popular attractions of the region. You may be in the sticks, but it feels much further away than that. ∎

**Tubac Golf Resort
P.O. Box 1297
Tubac, AZ 85646**

LOCATION: 40 minutes south of Tucson International Airport off Interstate 19.

ACCOMMODATIONS: 32 one- and two-room casitas and posadas.

DINING/ENTERTAINMENT: The Montura, rustic setting overlooking mountains with outstanding regional fare for breakfast, lunch and dinner; adjoining lounge.

AMENITIES: 18 holes of golf (Red Lawrence); one tennis court; swimming pool and spa; nature and hiking trails; horseback riding.

MEETING FACILITIES: 3,376 square feet of meeting space comprising a conference room and two smaller meeting rooms in Otero House.

RATES: Two-room casitas from $47; one-room posadas from $34.

RESERVATIONS: Call (800) 848-7893 or (602) 398-2211.

Places To Play

Tucson/Green Valley

Tucson

Arthur Pack Desert Golf Course
9101 N. Thornydale Road
Tucson, AZ 85741
(602) 744-3322
TYPE OF FACILITY: Public
NO. OF HOLES: 18
DESIGN: Desert
YARDAGE: 6,008-6,896
PAR: 72
PEAK RATES: $18. Cart optional.

Cliff Valley Golf Course
5910 N. Oracle Road
Tucson, AZ 85704
(602) 887-6161
TYPE OF FACILITY: Public Executive
NO. OF HOLES: 18
DESIGN: Traditional
YARDAGE: 2,261
PAR: 54
PEAK RATES: $5 for nine, $7.50 for 18. Cart optional.

Dorado Golf Course
6601 E. Speedway Blvd.
Tucson, AZ 85710
(602) 885-6751
TYPE OF FACILITY: Public Executive
NO. OF HOLES: 18
DESIGN: Traditional
YARDAGE: 3,360-4,000
PAR: 62
PEAK RATES: $14. Cart optional.

El Rio Golf Course
1400 W. Speedway Blvd.
Tucson, AZ 85745
(602) 623-6783
TYPE OF FACILITY: Public
NO. OF HOLES: 18
DESIGN: Desert
YARDAGE: 5,850-6,418
PAR: 70
PEAK RATES: $17. Cart optional.

Fred Enke Golf Course
8251 E. Irvington
Tucson, AZ 85730
(602) 296-8607
TYPE OF FACILITY: Public
NO. OF HOLES: 18
DESIGN: Desert
YARDAGE: 5,026-6,809
PAR: 72
PEAK RATES: $17. Cart optional.

Santa Rita Country Club
16461 S. Houghton Road
Tucson, AZ 85747
(602) 629-9717
TYPE OF FACILITY: Semi-private
NO. OF HOLES: 18
DESIGN: Traditional
YARDAGE: 5,565-6,329
PAR: 71
PEAK RATES: $15. Cart optional.

TPC at StarPass

Randolph Park Golf Courses
600 S. Alvernon Way
Tucson, AZ 85711
(602) 325-2811
TYPE OF FACILITY: Public
NO. OF HOLES: 36
DESIGN: Traditional
YARDAGE: North Course, 6,044-6,969;
South Course, 5,527-6,229
PAR: North Course, 72; South
Course, 70.
PEAK RATES: $19.50. Cart optional.
COMMENTS: Former site of PGA's
Tucson Open; Director of Golf is
Senior PGA Tour player Homero
Blancas.

TPC at StarPass

Silverbell Golf Course
3600 N. Silverbell Road
Tucson, AZ 85745
(602) 743-7284
TYPE OF FACILITY: Public
NO. OF HOLES: 18
DESIGN: Traditional
YARDAGE: 5,793-6,768
PAR: 72
PEAK RATES: $17. Cart optional.

Sun City Vistoso Golf Club
1495A E. Rancho Vistoso Blvd.
Tucson, AZ 85737
(602) 297-2033
TYPE OF FACILITY: Semi-private
NO. OF HOLES: 18
DESIGN: Desert
YARDAGE: 5,482-6,759
PAR: 72
PEAK RATES: $40. Cart included.

Tournament Players Club at StarPass
3645 W. 22nd Street
Tucson, AZ 85745
(602) 622-6060
TYPE OF FACILITY: Public
NO. OF HOLES: 18
DESIGN: Desert
YARDAGE: 5,210-7,010
PAR: 72
PEAK RATES: $65. Cart included.
COMMENTS: Stadium golf course; co-host of the PGA Tour's Tucson Open.

Green Valley

Canoa Hills Golf Course
1401 Calle Urbano
Green Valley, AZ 85614
(602) 648-1880
TYPE OF FACILITY: Public
NO. OF HOLES: 18
DESIGN: Desert
YARDAGE: 5,158-6,600
PAR: 72
PEAK RATES: $28. Cart included.

Haven Golf Course
110 N. Abrego
Green Valley, AZ 85614
(602) 625-4281
TYPE OF FACILITY: Public
NO. OF HOLES: 18
DESIGN: Traditional
YARDAGE: 5,811-6,829
PAR: 72
PEAK RATES: $16 for 18. Cart optional.

TPC at StarPass

San Ignacio Golf Club
24245 S. Camino del Sol
Green Valley, AZ 85614
(602) 648-3468
TYPE OF FACILITY: Public

NO. OF HOLES: 18
DESIGN: Desert
YARDAGE: 5,200-6,704
PAR: 72
PEAK RATES: $34. Cart included.

Other Arizona

Golf in Arizona isn't limited to expansive resorts with designer courses. In fact, visitors would be remiss not to venture outside the major resort areas and do a little exploring. There are many smaller golf-oriented resorts and hotels that offer tremendous vacation values. They may not offer the variety of the larger resorts in terms of amenities and services, but the price is right when it comes to clean and comfortable accommodations in a serene, relaxing environment. And best of all, the scenery is no different here than at the high-ticket resorts. Spend a few days among the red rocks at Sedona Golf Resort, or the towering Aspens at Fairfield Flagstaff Resort, and you'll get the message.

The adventure of an Arizona golf vacation can also be discovered at the hundreds of daily-fee and municipal golf courses throughout the state. If you're content to simply remain within the confines of your resort or hotel, you stand to miss some outstanding golf experiences such as Troon North in Scottsdale, The Foothills Golf Club in Phoenix, or the Karsten Course at Arizona State University at Tempe, all of which have been nationally recognized for excellence.

The following section will guide you to some of the state's outstanding smaller resorts, as well as its daily-fee and public-access golf courses. Take a few extra days, and check out some of these fine properties. You'll be glad you did.

Beaver Creek Golf Resort

LOCATED 90 MILES NORTH OF Phoenix off Interstate 17, in the sleepy town of Lake Montezuma, Beaver Creek Golf Resort is one of those unexplored, out-of-the-way places that most Arizonans wouldn't recognize. Hence lies the charm of the resort, which was once a part of the sprawling Bell Ranch (owned by Bell Telephone Systems).

The grassy pastures alongside Beaver Creek have since given way to the winding fairways and bentgrass greens of the Beaver Creek course, a traditional layout that plays 6,386 yards to a par of 71. The clubhouse, once the elegant ranch home that hosted Clark Gable, Carole Lombard and Betty Grable, radiates the warmth and earthiness of the turn-of-the-century Southwestern lifestyle. Guests overlook the golf course while breakfasting on freshly baked cinnamon rolls and, after a round of golf, indulge in a little fishing in the ponds scattered throughout the golf course (they're abundantly stocked with catfish, bass and bluegill).

Dinner at the clubhouse often includes Prime Rib (the house specialty), followed by a moonlit stroll to the Beaver Creek Inn with its cozy accommodations. The climate in these parts (typically 10 to 15 degrees cooler than the Phoenix area) adds to the resort's allure, as does its location. Beaver Creek Golf Resort is 25 minutes from Sedona, 45 minutes from Flagstaff and 90 minutes from the Grand Canyon. For those who enjoy golf and skiing and wish to truly "get away from it all," this is an ideal respite. ∎

Beaver Creek Golf Resort
P.O. Box 248
Lake Montezuma, AZ 86432

LOCATION: 90 miles north of Phoenix, off Interstate 17 (exit 293); 45 minutes from Flagstaff.

ACCOMMODATIONS: 22 rooms at Beaver Creek Inn.

DINING/ENTERTAINMENT: Golf clubhouse serves breakfast, lunch and dinner; adjacent lounge.

AMENITIES: 18 holes of golf, close to ski areas.

RATES: Guest rooms at Inn from $39; golf packages from $52.92.

RESERVATIONS: Call (602) 567-4487.

Rancho de los Caballeros

SO YOU'VE BEEN WONDERING where you could possibly wear those cowboy boots with spikes that the boys at the office gave you as a gag? While they may not work down at the club, they'd be perfect at Rancho de los Caballeros, an authentic, old-fashioned dude ranch just outside the old mining town of Wickenburg, some 55 miles northwest of Phoenix. This 20,000-acre spread is both a hospitable guest ranch and a thriving working ranch, welcoming guests from early fall to late spring to enjoy a variety of rustic yet eminently comfortable accommodations, three meals daily on the American Plan, and an array of recreational opportunities.

While horseback riding is certainly an activity of choice (the ranch's 60-horse stable is one of the finest around, and a guided exploration of nearby Vulture Mine is requisite), golf has become immensely popular here, thanks to a fine desert-style 18-hole course. Ranked among the country's top 75 resort courses by *Golf Digest*, the Rancho de

los Caballeros Golf Club stretches 7,025 yards from the tips (with a 134 slope), and is open only to members and guests of the ranch.

The course, unlike the ranch, is open year-round and is kept in excellent condition throughout the year. This is a big hitter's course, and Rancho de los Caballeros is a big eater's paradise with excellent "home cookin" that ranges from griddle cakes at breakfast to a buffet luncheon at poolside (all baked goods are prepared on site) to an elegant and intimate dinner in the ranch's main dining room. Accommodations range from standard rooms to bungalows with working fireplaces and refrigerators to suites of more than 2,500 square feet of living space.

Rancho de los Caballeros provides an opportunity to escape to an earlier, less complicated era, when earning the trust of a faithful mount meant more than meeting deadlines. Bring your family, and bring an appetite for adventure as well as good chow. And bring your boots—spikes optional. ∎

Rancho de los Caballeros
P.O. Box 1148
Wickenburg, AZ 85358

LOCATION: 55 miles northwest of Phoenix off Highway 60, two miles west of Wickenburg. Private aircraft have access to Wickenburg Municipal Airport.

ACCOMMODATIONS: 40 Sun Terrace (standard) rooms, 12 Sunset Rooms (bungalows), 22 Bradshaw Suites.

DINING/ENTERTAINMENT: The ranch operates on the American Plan (breakfast, lunch and dinner daily), which is included in the room charge. Meals are normally served in the main dining room, but arrangements may be made for meals to be served poolside, in the Bar Patio or in the Palo Verde Conference Center. Complete food and beverage service available in Golf Club's dining room.

AMENITIES: 18 holes of golf (Greg Nash & Jeff Hardin); swimming; four acrylic tennis courts; horseback riding; skeet and trap shooting; Western cookouts and hayrides.

MEETING FACILITIES: 9,500 square feet of meeting space including 4,500-square-foot Palo Verde Conference Center.

RATES: Sun Terrace (standard) rooms from $210, Sunset Room bungalows from $230, and Bradshaw Suites from $260.

RESERVATIONS: Open October through May. Call (602) 684-5484.

Places To Play

Flagstaff/Sedona

Flagstaff

Fairfield Flagstaff Resort
(Elden Hills Golf Club)
2380 N. Oakmont Drive
Flagstaff, AZ 86004
(602) 527-7999
TYPE OF FACILITY: Public Resort
NO. OF HOLES: 18
DESIGN: Traditional
YARDAGE: 5,380-6,104
PAR: 73
PEAK RATES: $38. Cart mandatory on weekends.
COMMENTS: Part of condominium resort surrounded by millions of acres of national forest.

Pinewood Country Club
P.O. Box 584
Munds Park, AZ 86017
(602) 286-1110
TYPE OF FACILITY: Semi-private
NO. OF HOLES: 18
DESIGN: Traditional
YARDAGE: 5,342-6,434
PAR: 72
PEAK RATES: $40. Cart included.

Sedona Golf Resort

Payson/Overgaard

Pine Meadows Country Club
Country Club Drive, P.O. Box 562
Overgaard, AZ 85933
(602) 535-4220
TYPE OF FACILITY: Semi-private
NO. OF HOLES: 9

DESIGN: Traditional
YARDAGE: 2,340-2,631
PAR: 34
PEAK RATES: $9 for nine, $16 for 18.
Cart optional.
COMMENTS: Nine holes recently added.

Sedona/Verde Valley

Canyon Mesa Country Club
500 Jacks Canyon Road
Sedona, AZ 86336
(602) 284-2176
TYPE OF FACILITY: Semi-private
Executive
NO. OF HOLES: 9
DESIGN: Traditional
YARDAGE: 1,010-1,475
PAR: 28
PEAK RATES: $15. Cart optional.

Oak Creek Country Club
690 Bell Rock Blvd.
Sedona, AZ 86336
(602) 284-1660
TYPE OF FACILITY: Semi-private
Resort
NO. OF HOLES: 18
DESIGN: Traditional
YARDAGE: 5,555-6,880
PAR: 72
PEAK RATES: $40. Cart included.

Sedona Golf Resort
7256 Highway 179
Sedona, AZ 86336
(602) 284-9355
TYPE OF FACILITY: Semi-private
Resort
NO. OF HOLES: 18
DESIGN: Links
YARDAGE: 5,637-6,642
PAR: 71
PEAK RATES: $40. Cart included.

COMMENTS: Excellent Gary Panks design, with lush green fairways spread among the red rocks. Subtle elevation and terrain changes. Awe-inspiring scenery; perhaps one of the prettiest courses in the U.S. Part of a residential and resort community; plans include, among other amenities, a 160-room luxury hotel.

Sedona Golf Resort

Poco Diablo Resort
S. Highway 179, Box 1709
Sedona, AZ 86336
(602) 282-7333, ext. 135
Type of Facility: Public/Resort
Executive
No. of Holes: Nine
Design: Traditional
Yardage: 720
Par: 27
Peak Rates: $12. Walking only.

Verde Valley Country Club
P.O Box 458,
Country Club Road
Clarkdale, AZ 86324
(602) 634-5491
Type of Facility: Semi-private
No. of Holes: Nine
Design: Traditional
Yardage: 2,907-3,193
Par: 36
Peak Rates: $15. Cart optional.

Williams

**The Elephant Rocks Golf Course
at Williams**
2200 Country Club Drive
Williams, AZ 86046
(602) 635-4936
Type of Facility: Public

No. of Holes: Nine
Design: Traditional
Yardage: 2,527-3,100
Par: 35
Peak Rates: $10 for nine, $16 for 18.
Cart optional.

Nevada

Las Vegas

Contrary to popular opinion, Las Vegas is not America's last bastion of decadence. Nevada's largest city deserves a better fate than to be associated solely with Bugsy Siegel, Howard Hughes and Wayne Newton. In reality, there are a lot of truly great things about Vegas. Consider that the city has more than 74,000 hotels rooms and still enjoys greater than an 85-percent year-round occupancy rate. Conventions and meetings brought more than $1 billion to the city's economy last year. Las Vegas is the seat of Clark County, which offers its 700,000 residents one of the fastest-growing school districts in the country. This is not only the Entertainment Capital of the World, hosting more than 20 million visitors annually, it's one of the world's great success stories as well.

Las Vegas is, for all intents and purposes, the "Strip," a 3 1/2-mile stretch of glitter, glamour, pageantry and boundless 24-hour activity. The resort hotels here are as legendary as their casinos, and there's seemingly no end in sight to the area's staggering growth. Scheduled for a 1993 opening is the $1 billion MGM Grand Hotel and Theme Park, the largest hotel in the world (5,007 rooms, surpassing the 4,032 rooms at the Excaliber, located just across the street) and family-oriented theme park. Yes, Vegas has taken a turn toward family-oriented entertainment. In fact, one of the Strip's most popular attractions hasn't a slot machine or gaming table. It is Wet 'N Wild, a 16-acre water theme park built in 1985 on an expensive piece of land next to the Sahara Hotel. Gaming insiders wrote off the project before it was completed, but for the past eight years the park has attracted more than a half-million visitors annually.

Recreational pursuits have also become an integral part of the Las Vegas experience, and golf is certainly included. The Desert Inn, one of the Strip's venerable landmarks, is one of the few properties in the country that has hosted PGA, LPGA and PGA Senior tour events. In fact, the tradition of big money golf tournaments in Vegas got its start at the Desert Inn in 1953, when owner Wilbur Clark put up 10,000 silver dollars for the winner of the first Tournament of Champions. The story has it that champ Al Besselink lost it all in the casino before sunset.

In addition to its professional tournaments, the Las Vegas area hosts one of the richest state opens, a national junior tournament and a perennial nationally ranked college team. It has also turned out players like Robert Gamez and Tommy Armour III, both of whom have won PGA Tour events, and LPGA Tour pro Deborah McHaffie. Yet despite all the makings of a hotbed of golf, the area still suffers from a shortage of public-access courses. Such growth is hampered by the scarcity of available land and high construction costs. Because topsoil is scarce and irrigation costs are high, it's not unusual for a course to run as much as $10 million.

Thankfully, some relief appears to be on the horizon. Boasting only 12 courses seven years ago, Las Vegas can expect to have as many as 30 by 1995 if several proposed projects reach fruition. With the burgeoning population of Clark County, and the growing number of golf hungry visitors coming to the area, Vegas may be on its way toward following the lead of its Palm Springs and Arizona neighbors. But one thing is sure: Once you find a course to play in Vegas, you'll never have trouble finding a game. And if you hear the word "pigeon" bandied about by your partners, you're probably better off back at the casino.

Getting There

McCarran International, one of the nation's busiest and fastest growing airports, is located just one mile from the Las Vegas Strip, three miles from the Convention Center and five miles from downtown. Twenty commercial and commuter airlines provide regular daily service, and all major rental car companies are represented at the airport. Virtually every resort hotel in town offers transportation to and from the airport—some for free, others for a nominal charge.

Weather

Las Vegas has an arid climate, with an average of 310 days of sunshine per year and an average annual rainfall of just 4.19 inches. Daytime temperatures may reach more than 100 degrees during the summer months, June through September. Spring and fall are relatively short with temperatures in the 70s while the winter months have daytime temperatures in the 50s and 60s.

Activities

If you do manage to make it out of the casino, you'll find that Las Vegas actually serves as a gateway for some of the most scenic country in the Western U.S. A nice break from the lush green of the gaming tables is Red Rock Canyon, a 400-million-year-old sea of blazing rock formations, located 11 miles west of town. At  the base of Red Rock Canyon is Spring Mountain Ranch, an oasis of high desert flora and fauna once owned by Howard Hughes. Also nearby is Bonnie Springs Ranch and Old Nevada, a re-creation of the Old West with gunslingers, stagecoaches, an opera house and restaurant. To the Southeast is Hoover Dam, an engineering marvel that holds back the Colorado River to form the 100-mile-long Lake Mead. With an incredible 550 miles of shoreline, Lake Mead offers swimming, water skiing and boating as well as rafting on the Colorado. Back in town, the 10,000-seat Cashman Field is home to the Las Vegas Stars, the AAA affiliate of the San Diego Padres.

Attractions

In addition to the Strip itself, there's the aforementioned Wet 'N Wild, Ripley's Believe It Or Not Museum, the Guinness World of Records Museum, and the Imperial Palace Auto Collection, an intriguing array of more than 200 antique and classic cars. Kids will also go for tours through the Ethel M Chocolate Factory (the "M" is for Mars, the bar which Ethel created), as well as the Southern Nevada Zoological Park, a charming zoo just five minutes from downtown. Two museums of note are the Las Vegas Museum of Natural History and the Clark County Heritage Museum in nearby Henderson, which offers a taste of what the Old West was really like.

Dining

From charbroiled hot dogs to chateaubriand, dining in Las Vegas is a truly unique experience. Prices vary from as much as $75 per person at a gourmet restaurant on the Strip to as little as $2.95 for a buffet in the same hotel. You can find prime rib dinners with all the trimmings for $5.95, steak and lobster for less than $8, and all-you-can-eat ribs for $5.95. Then again, the bird's nest soup at the Empress Court in Caesers Palace will run you $56 for two. While the Mirage and Excalibur hotels both have a variety of excellent dining experiences, there are several fine "off-Strip" restaurants. Among them: the Bamboo Garden for simple, elegant Chinese dining in a relaxed atmosphere; the Aristocrat, serving Continental with a warm ambience; Jerome's, a taste of San Francisco in both cuisine and decor; and Pamplemousse, with fine French country dishes and atmosphere that has gotten raves from *Bon Appetit* and *Playboy.*

Shopping

Located in the heart of the Strip is The Fashion Show Mall, a shopping mecca that boasts high fashion department stores such as Saks Fifth Avenue and Neiman-Marcus as well as more than 140 specialty shops such as Banana Republic, The Sharper Image and Units. Three miles from the Strip, the Boulevard Mall offers four major department stores and a large selection of variety stores. Further out of town is The Meadows Mall, stretching over 85 acres and offering a plethora of department stores and specialty shops, restaurants and snack bars.

For More Information

Las Vegas Convention and Visitors Authority, 3150 Paradise Road, Las Vegas, NV 89109, (702) 892-0711.

Desert Inn

The legendary leader of the Vegas Strip

IT WAS APRIL 1950, AND THE BRAND-spanking-new Desert Inn on the Las Vegas Strip had already turned this fledgling desert playground on its ear. With 350 employees, the Desert Inn was the largest employer in Nevada, and its three-story tower was the tallest building on the Strip. Opening night in the Painted Desert Room (now the Crystal Room) featured a stellar lineup of stars: Edgar Bergen and Charlie McCarthy, Vivian Blaine, Les Chalivels, the Ray Noble Orchestra and the Arden Fletcher Dancers.

Much has changed up and down the Strip, the Desert Inn notwithstanding. A number of owners have come and gone, including a rather reclusive chap named Hughes, but the resort has continued to thrive as one of the Strip's most luxurious destinations. As a self-contained resort, it is unique among the other hotel/casinos in Las Vegas. It has also enjoyed 14 years as a member of Preferred Hotels of the World, a group of 70 upper-echelon hotels and resorts around the globe. The stars continue to flock through the resort's Crystal Room, but just as many can be found on the fairways of the Desert Inn golf course.

Golf arrived at the Desert Inn in 1952, and it became the home of the Tournament of Champions the following year. Sam Snead, Gene Littler, Arnold Palmer and Jack Nicklaus were among the winners here who accepted their prize money in the form of silver dollars, the area's currency of choice. The tournament left in 1966, but pro golf returned to the Desert Inn in 1983 in the form of the big-money Las Vegas Invitational. It remains part of the tournament's rotation today, as well as having been the host of the PGA Senior Tour's Las Vegas Senior Classic—an annual reunion of many of the original Tournament of Champions participants—and the LPGA's Desert Inn International. From 1980 to '85 it was the site of the LPGA's J&B Scotch Pro-Am, whose winners' roll included Nancy Lopez, Patty Sheehan, Pat Bradley and Ayako Okamoto.

This is a flat but long golf course (7,111 yards) with several tough holes

that bolster the track's 75.2 rating from the tips. Most notorious is the stretch from the seventh to the ninth holes. The seventh is the sternest test on the course, a 205-yard par-three surrounded by sand and water. Throughout the '80s this hole ranked as the second hardest par-three on the PGA Tour, second only to the legendary 16th at Cypress Point.

Then comes a pair of nasty par-fours, the 442-yard eighth and the 432-yard ninth, both of which play to large, well-protected greens. The most interesting holes on the back nine require dead aim off the tee: the 411-yard, par-four 14th is a dogleg left with a fairway bunker in the prime landing area, while the 395-yard, par-four 17th serves up fairway bunkers to the left, water to the right and trees in the middle. Hitting driver is a gamble here; something along the lines of an 8-iron might be more appropriate.

Of course, if you want to find the real gamblers, look in the club's 19th hole or over in the hotel's casino, a showplace that enjoyed an extensive renovation in 1978. The race and sports book is also a good bet (pun intended), with 1,800 square feet and 13 television monitors to view sporting

events from virtually all major arenas.

Winnings may be spent in a variety of ways, from the Desert Inn Shopping Arcade to one of the resort's fine restaurants (try the Nevada quail in red wine sauce in the elegant Monte Carlo Room, or the famous Peking duck in Ho Wan, whose name translates to "good fortune").

Those less enamored with gaming (but then again, why would you be *here*?) can take solace in the 18,000-square-foot Desert Inn Spa, which offers the full menu of fitness programs and skin care services, as well as an adjacent jogging track.

Howard Hughes played a storied part in the history of the Desert Inn. In 1967 Hughes bought the resort through the Hughes Tool Company, which later became Summa Corp., the largest private landowner in Nevada. On Nov. 27, 1970, exactly four years from the date of his entrance, Hughes left the Desert Inn for the last time.

It is this mystique, along with the allure of the resort's outstanding facilities and its lasting reputation for excellence, that keeps guests coming back. ■

Desert Inn Hotel & CC
Las Vegas, Nevada

LOCATION: 3145 Las Vegas Blvd. South, Las Vegas, NV 89109; 10 min. from airport.

ACCOMMODATIONS: 821 rooms and suites.

DINING/ENTERTAINMENT: Monte Carlo, gourmet cuisine; Portofino, northern Italian fare; Ho Wan, authentic Cantonese, Mandarin and Szechuan cuisine; La Promenade, American and Continental dishes served 24 hours; Champions Deli; Pool Bar; Starlight Theatre Lounge; Casino Bar.

AMENITIES: 18 holes of golf; 10 tennis courts; swimming pool; 10 hydrowhirl spas; health spa; jogging and exercise track; casino; race/sports book; retail/specialty shops.

MEETING FACILITIES: More than 42,000 square feet of divisible space including two large indoor ballrooms and a 12,000-square-foot poolside patio.

RATES: Guest rooms from $90; suites from $150 to $325.

RESERVATIONS: Call (800) 634-6906.

Places To Play

Las Vegas/ Southern Nevada

Las Vegas

Angel Park Golf Club
100 S. Rampart Blvd.
Las Vegas, NV 89128
(702) 254-4653
Type of Facility: Municipal
No. OF HOLES: 36
YEAR OPENED: 1989
YARDAGE: Palm Course, 5,790-6,120; Mountain Course, 5,147-6,235
PAR: Palm Course, Women 70, Men 71; Mountain Course, 71
RATES: Residents, $25 weekdays, $30 weekends; non-residents, $50. Carts included.
COMMENTS: Both Arnold Palmer designs. Palm features rugged, terrain with fast, bentgrass greens. Mountain offers views of Las Vegas and Red Rock area. Also features an 18-hole lighted putting course.

Desert Rose Country Club
5843 Club House Drive
Las Vegas, NV 89122
(702) 438-4653
TYPE OF FACILITY: Municipal
No. OF HOLES: 18
YEAR OPENED: 1960
YARDAGE: 5,458-6,600
PAR: 71
RATES: Residents, $5.75 for nine, $10.50 for 18; non-residents, $11.75 for nine, $21.50 for 18. Carts optional.
COMMENTS: Formerly known as Winterwood Golf Course, Desert Rose features moderate length, plush fairways and moderate to fast greens. The course record of 64 is held by Senior PGA touring pro and course operator Jim Colbert.

Dunes Country Club
3650 Las Vegas Blvd. South
Las Vegas, NV 89109
(702) 737-4746
TEE TIMES: (702) 737-4749
TYPE OF FACILITY: Resort
NO. OF HOLES: 18
YEAR OPENED: 1964
YARDAGE: 5,982-7,240
PAR: 72
RATES: Hotel guests, $60
weekdays, $70 weekends; non-guests, $70 weekdays, $80
weekends; local residents, $50.
COMMENTS: Long, difficult desert
layout with many palm trees.
Part of Dunes Hotel & Casino
complex.

Las Vegas Golf Club
4349 Vegas Drive
Las Vegas, NV 89108
(702) 646-3003
TYPE OF FACILITY: Municipal
NO. OF HOLES: 18
YEAR OPENED: 1949
YARDAGE: 5,715-6,631
PAR: 72
RATES: Residents, $8.50; non-residents, $11. Nine-hole rates
vary seasonally. Carts optional.
COMMENTS: Very mature course
with lots of trees and little water.
Operated by Senior PGA Tour
pro Jim Colbert. PGA Tour's
Robert Gamez grew up playing
here.

Los Prados Country Club
5150 Los Prados Circle
Las Vegas, NV 89130
(702) 645-5696
TYPE OF FACILITY: Semi-private
NO. OF HOLES: 18
YEAR OPENED: 1985
YARDAGE: 5,000-5,500
PAR: 70
RATES: Residents, $7; non-residents, $17 ($8.50 after 3 p.m.).
Carts optional.
COMMENTS: Short and tight, Los
Prados is well bunkered with fast
greens. Lots of trees and out-of-bounds, with course bordering
desert.

Painted Desert Golf Course
5555 Painted Mirage Way
Las Vegas, NV 89129
(702) 645-2568
TYPE OF FACILITY: Public
NO. OF HOLES: 18
YEAR OPENED: 1987
YARDAGE: 5,711-6,840
PAR: 72
RATES: Residents, $33 weekdays,
$38 weekends; non-residents,
$50. Special twilight rates (after
2:30 p.m.) available. Carts
included.
COMMENTS: Excellent desert target
course designed by Jay Morrish.
Lush fairway landing pads amid
natural desert landscape.

Painted Desert Golf Course

Sahara Country Club
1911 E. Desert Inn Road
Las Vegas, NV 89109
(702) 796-0013
TYPE OF FACILITY: Public
NO. OF HOLES: 18
YEAR OPENED: 1961
YARDAGE: 5,761-6,815
PAR: 71
RATES: Residents, $40; non-residents, $60. Carts included.
COMMENTS: Mature, established course with olive, palm and evergreen trees. Co-hosted the Tournament of Champions from '62-'67; also hosted Sahara Invitational in early '70s. Par-five 18th hole is one of the best finishing holes in the area.

Sun City Summerlin Golf Club
9201-B Del Webb Blvd.
Las Vegas, NV 89128
(702) 363-4373
TYPE OF FACILITY: Semi-private
NO. OF HOLES: 18
YEAR OPENED: 1989
YARDAGE: 5,502-6,940
PAR: 72
RATES: Residents, $21 for nine, $36 for 18; non-residents, $30 for 9, $54 for 18. Lower summer rates available. Cart included.
COMMENTS: A tough course on rolling, wide-open terrain. Heavily bunkered bentgrass greens. Course will close to the public when membership reaches sell-out.

Sunrise Vista Golf Course
Building T 1619
Nellis Air Force Base, NV 89191
(702) 652-2602
TYPE OF FACILITY: Public
NO. OF HOLES: 18
YEAR OPENED: 1972
YARDAGE: 5,506-6,813
PAR: 72

RATES: Weekdays, $10 for nine,
$12 for 18; Weekends, $12 for
nine, $14 for 18. Sliding scale for
military. Carts optional.
COMMENTS: Government-owned
course formerly known as Nellis
Golf Course. Flat course with four
lakes. Not hard to find - get on the
base and ask an MP for directions.

North Las Vegas

Craig Ranch Golf Course
628 W. Craig Road
North Las Vegas, NV 89129
(702) 642-9700
TYPE OF FACILITY: Public

NO. OF HOLES: 18
YARDAGE: 5,221-6,000
PAR: 70
RATES: $6.50 for nine, $10 for 18.
Carts optional.

Legacy Golf Club

North Las Vegas Golf Course
324 E. Brooks
North Las Vegas, NV 89036
(702) 649-7171
TYPE OF FACILITY: Municipal Par-Three
NO. OF HOLES: Nine
YEAR OPENED: 1972
YARDAGE: 1,158

PAR: 27
RATES: Weekdays, $3, seniors $2, students, $2.50; weekends, $4; slightly higher for night play.
COMMENTS: Only lighted course in Nevada. Night views of Las Vegas. Last tee time 10 p.m.; course closes about midnight.

Henderson/Green Valley

Black Mountain Golf & CC
501 Country Club Drive
Henderson, NV 89015
(702) 565-7933
TYPE OF FACILITY: Semi-private
NO. OF HOLES: 18

YARDAGE: 5,714-6,775
PAR: Women 74, Men 72
FEES: Weekdays, $11 for nine, $15 for 18; weekends, $15 for nine, $20 for 18. Carts mandatory on weekends until noon.

Las Vegas Indian Wells CC
1 Country Club Drive
Henderson, NV 89014
(702) 451-2106
TYPE OF FACILITY: Semi-private
NO. OF HOLES: 18
YARDAGE: 5,275-6,913
PAR: Women 72, Men 71
RATES: Non-residents: $45.50 for nine, $50 for 18. Carts included. Twilight rates available.
COMMENTS: Hilly, mature links-type course that hosted the Panasonic Las Vegas PGA Tour event in 1984 and '85.

Legacy Golf Club
130 Par Excellence Dr.
Henderson, NV 89016
(702) 897-2187
TYPE OF FACILITY: Public
NO. OF HOLES: 18
YEAR OPENED: 1989
YARDAGE: 5,340-7,150
PAR: 72
RATES: Weekdays, $55; weekends, $60. Cart included.
COMMENTS: Excellent link-type course designed by Arthur Hills. Many forced carries over desert landscape. Very well maintained.

Painted Desert Golf Course

Boulder City

Boulder City Municipal Golf Course
1 Clubhouse Drive
Boulder City, NV 89005
(702) 293-9236
TYPE OF FACILITY: Municipal
NO. OF HOLES: 18
YEAR OPENED: 1972

YARDAGE: 5,566-6,561
PAR: 72
RATES: $9 for nine, $15 for 18. Carts optional.
COMMENTS: Fairly flat desert course. Unusually good condition year-round for a muni.

Laughlin

Emerald River Country Club
1155 Casino Drive
Laughlin, NV 89029
(702) 298-0061
TYPE OF FACILITY: Resort
NO. OF HOLES: 18
YEAR OPENED: 1990
YARDAGE: 5,205-6,809

PAR: 72
RATES: Laughlin-area resort/casino guests: weekdays, $27.50 for nine, $55 for 18; weekends, $32.50, $65. Carts included.
COMMENTS: Championship-caliber course on the Colorado River. Difficult, with narrow fairways.

Moapa Valley

Arcadian Greens
State Route 169, Box 82
Loganville, NV 89021
(702) 397-2431
TYPE OF FACILITY: Public
NO. OF HOLES: Nine
YEAR OPENED: 1990

YARDAGE: 3,215
PAR: 37
RATES: $7, $6 for seniors, $5 for students.
COMMENTS: Water in play on four holes. New nine scheduled for completion by mid-1990s.

Mesquite

Peppermill Palms Golf Course
2200 Hillside Drive
Mesquite, NV 89024
(702) 346-5232 or (800) 621-0187
TYPE OF FACILITY: Resort
NO. OF HOLES: 18
YEAR OPENED: 1989
YARDAGE: 4,950-6,880
PAR: 72
RATES: Resort guests, $30 weekdays,

$40 weekends; non-guests, $40 weekdays, $45 weekends. Local residents, $35 anytime. Carts included.
COMMENTS: Front side is desert layout with 27 acres of water; back nine is hilly with up to 140-foot drops from some tees to fairways. Associated with nearby Peppermill Hotel & Casino.

Pahrump

Calvada Valley Golf & CC
Box 220
Pahrump, NV 89041
(702) 727-4653
TYPE OF FACILITY: Public
NO. OF HOLES: 18
YEAR OPENED: 1980
YARDAGE: 5,914-7,036
PAR: Women 73, Men 71
RATES: $15 for nine, $30 for 18. Carts included.

Calvada Executive Golf Club
Box 220
Pahrump, NV 89041
(702) 727-6388
TYPE OF FACILITY: Public Executive
NO. OF HOLES: 18
YEAR OPENED: 1984
YARDAGE: 3,222-3,587
PAR: Women 60, Men 59
RATES: $6 for nine, $12 for 18. No carts.

Reno/Tahoe

To be perfectly candid, Reno and Lake Tahoe are two very good reasons why you would never go back to Las Vegas. Centrally located along Nevada's western border, the area's stunning Alpine mountain vistas and green, fertile valleys are a welcome contrast to the stark desert surroundings of Vegas. And rest assured that there is no shortage of activity in the Reno/Tahoe area, from the gaming tables to the area's magnificent golf courses.

Reno has been called "the Biggest Little City in the World," a smaller, friendlier, prettier alternative to Las Vegas. Even the casinos tend to be more accommodating to recreational players. Gambling remains the city's No. 1 attraction, although summer golf and winter skiing are becoming increasingly popular.

Lake Tahoe is one of the finest year-round resorts in the world, with internationally renowned skiing in the winter and water sports and golf dominating the spring and summer months. One of the best ways to experience Lake Tahoe—the largest Alpine lake in North America and the second deepest—is to drive the 72 miles around it. The 28-mile drive along the Nevada shore, from the California-Nevada state line to Crystal Bay, is a special treat. Along the way is Stateline, a major casino center with a number of excellent resort hotels. A short distance east is Friday's Station, which in pioneer times was a famous stop on the Pony Express. Today the area is more famous for its golf courses; most notably Edgewood Tahoe, regarded as perhaps the finest public course in the U.S.

History, beauty and an abundance of year-round activity make the Reno/Tahoe area the state's great alternative for vacationers. It's hardly Nevada's best-kept secret, but it certainly seems that way.

Getting There

The area is serviced by Reno-Cannon International Airport, a five-minute drive from downtown Reno. American, Continental, Delta, USAir, United and America West are the major airlines. Rental cars and airport transportation are available.

Weather

The Reno/Tahoe region averages 350 inches of snow annually and winter temperatures from 25 to 45 degrees. The area also gets sunshine most of the year; temperatures range in the 70s and 80s during this period.

Attractions

Reno: Circus Circus, a children's attraction at the resort/casino with circus acts and a carnival-type midway; and Fleischmann Planetarium on the University of Nevada-Reno campus. Sparks: Wild Island, a family entertainment complex and water park. Virginia City: The Delta Saloon and the Bucket of Blood Saloon, restored Old West watering holes; and the Virginia and Truckee Railroad, with daily trips on the steam-powered train through the city's old mining area. Lake Tahoe: The Ponderosa Ranch, site of the long-time television series *Bonanza*.

Dining

Reno: Harrah's Steak House, dark and romantic and away from the bustling casino; Rapscallion Seafood House and Bar, a traditional French restaurant; and La Strada, exceptional Italian fare in the Eldorado Casino. North Tahoe: Hugos, a Hyatt restaurant with the best views on the lake's north shore; and The Soule Domain, a cozy 1927 pine-log cabin with creative fare. South Tahoe: Empress Court, elegant Chinese at Caesars Tahoe Resort; and Sage Room Steak House, elegant dining at Harvey's Casino.

For More Information

Reno/Sparks Convention and Visitors Authority, 4590 S. Virginia St., Reno, NV 89504, (702) 827-7366 or (800) 367-7366. Reno-Tahoe Visitors Center, 135 N. Sierra St., Reno, NV 89504, (702) 348-7788.

Places To Play

Reno/Lake Tahoe

Edgewood Tahoe

Reno/Sparks

Brookside Golf Course
700 S. Rock Boulevard
Reno, NV 89502
(702) 322-6009
TYPE OF FACILITY: Municipal
NO. OF HOLES: Nine
YEAR OPENED: 1956
YARDAGE: 2,502-2,882
PAR: 35

RATES: $3.50 for 9, $6 for 18. Discounts available for seniors and students. Carts optional. **COMMENTS:** Flat, open course with water and bunkers on several holes. Originally an 18-hole course, but one nine was acquired for Reno airport expansion. Thus, the roar of jet aircraft is common.

Lakeridge Golf Course
1200 Razorback Road
Reno, NV 89509
(702) 825-2200
TYPE OF FACILITY: Semi-private
NO. OF HOLES: 18
YEAR OPENED: 1969
YARDAGE: 5,159-6,717
PAR: 72
RATES: $44 for 18, $25 after 3 p.m.,

$15 for walkers after 5:30 p.m. Cart included. Fees lower in early spring and late fall. **COMMENTS:** Robert Trent Jones, Jr., design with large greens, bunkers and a lot of water. The 15th hole, a 239-yard par-3, drops 143 feet from the blue tees to an island green in Lake Stanley. Open March through December.

Northgate Golf Course
1111 Clubhouse Drive
Reno, NV 89523
(702) 747-7577
TYPE OF FACILITY: Resort
NO. OF HOLES: 18
YEAR OPENED: 1988
YARDAGE: 5,521-6,966
PAR: 72
RATES: $20 for 9 after 2 p.m., $35

for 18. Carts included. **COMMENTS:** Challenging, desert links-style course with undulating fairways and large greens guarded by both sand and grass bunkers. Only course in Nevada to host U.S. Open qualifying in '88 and '89. Former stop on the Ben Hogan Tour. Open February 1 through December 15.

Sierra Sage Golf Course
6355 Silver Lake Blvd.
Stead, NV 89506
(702) 972-1564
TYPE OF FACILITY: Municipal
NO. OF HOLES: 18
YEAR OPENED: 1958
YARDAGE: 5,573-6,623
PAR: 71
RATES: $7.50 for nine, $12 for 18.
Reduced fees for seniors and
students. Carts optional.
COMMENTS: Built by the U.S. Air
Force. Links-style course with
sagebrush lining generous,
rolling fairways. Water, sand
bunkers, and small greens.

Washoe County Golf Course
2601 S. Arlington
Reno, NV 89509
(702) 785-4286
TYPE OF FACILITY: Municipal
NO. OF HOLES: 18
YEAR OPENED: 1934
YARDAGE: 5,973-6,695
PAR: Women 74, Men 72
RATES: $12. Reduced fees for
seniors and students. Carts
optional.
COMMENTS: Mature, well-estab-
lished course. Front nine is flat,
back nine is hilly. Tall trees
border the fairways, and bunkers
crowd the small greens.

Incline Village Golf Course

Wildcreek Golf Course
3500 Sullivan Lane
Sparks, NV 89431
(702) 673-3100
TYPE OF FACILITY: Resort
NO. OF HOLES: 18 Regulation, nine Executive
YEAR OPENED: 1979
YARDAGE: Championship Course, 5,472-6,932; Executive Course, 2,340-2,840
PAR: Championship Course, 72; Executive Course, 27.
RATES: Championship Course, $20 for nine after 2 p.m., $35 for 18. Carts included. Reduced fees in winter when walking is allowed. Executive Course, $8 for nine, $10 for 18. Reduced fees in winter. No carts.
COMMENTS: Championship Course is very hilly with lots of water, bunkers, and sagebrush. Hosted Gatlin Brothers Senior PGA Tour event in '82 and '83. Open February through December. Executive Course features rolling hills and lots of water, but wide fairways and large greens. Challenging par-three course, but great for beginners. Open all year.

South Tahoe

Edgewood Tahoe

Edgewood Tahoe
180 Lake Parkway
Stateline, NV 89449
(702) 588-3566
TYPE OF FACILITY: Resort
NO. OF HOLES: 18
YEAR OPENED: 1968
YARDAGE: 5,749-7,491
PAR: 72
RATES: $100. Carts included.
COMMENTS: One of the top 100 courses in the country, and the most difficult course in Nevada. Extremely long, built on a lush lakeshore meadow. Hosted the U.S. Senior Open in 1985, the Publinks in 1980, and the Lake Tahoe Classic, a senior tour pro-am event, in 1989. A "must-play" in this neck of the woods, despite the high fee. Open May through October.

Glenbrook Golf Course
Pray Meadow Road
Glenbrook, NV 89413
(702) 749-5201
TYPE OF FACILITY: Resort
NO. OF HOLES: Nine
YEAR OPENED: 1926
YARDAGE: 4,872-5,318 (based on 18 holes)
PAR: Women 72, Men 71.
RATES: $22 for nine, $30 for 18. After 2 p.m., $22 unlimited play. Before June 15 and after Sept. 15, $22 unlimited play. Carts optional.
COMMENTS: Nevada's oldest course, named by *Golf Digest* one of the finest nine-hole courses in the world. Course-record 62 set by Ben Hogan in 1950. Picturesque third green framed by Lake Tahoe. Open mid-April through mid-October.

North Tahoe

Incline Golf Course (Championship)
955 Fairway Blvd.
Incline Village, NV 89450
(702) 832-1144
TYPE OF FACILITY: Resort
NO. OF HOLES: 18
YEAR OPENED: 1964
YARDAGE: 5,365-6,910
PAR: 72
RATES: Residents $33, $17 after 4 p.m.; non-residents $75, $30 after 4 p.m. Carts included.
COMMENTS: Classic design by Robert Trent Jones Sr. Open May through October.

Incline Golf Course (Executive)
690 Wilson Way
Incline Village, NV 89450
(702) 832-1150
TYPE OF FACILITY: Resort Executive
NO. OF HOLES: 18
YEAR OPENED: 1973
YARDAGE: 3,002-3,513
PAR: 58
RATES: Residents, $22, $15 after 4 p.m.; non-residents, $40, $22 after 4 p.m. Carts included.
COMMENTS: Robert Trent Jones Jr. design rated among the top executive courses in the U.S.

New Mexico

New Mexico is known as the Land of Enchantment, where the sun sets with a magical show of light and double rainbows stretch across the sky after a heavy rain. Indeed, this is a place whose assets are its natural treasures, from the Santa Fe Trail and the Rio Grande, to ancient Indian ruins and dusty streets where Billy the Kid stirred many a fracas. It is also a land of warm, friendly people whose traditions and cultures are steeped in history.

While many of us have never considered a vacation in New Mexico, the cultural and recreational opportunities are virtually limitless. The climate is perfect year-round for outdoor activity; in fact, before being known as the Land of Enchantment, New Mexico went by the nickname the Sunshine State (with apologies to Florida, of course), based on the fact that every part of the state receives at least 70 percent sunshine year-round. Because of its size, however, the climate varies dramatically from one region to another. For instance, snowfall ranges from less than two inches annually in the lower Rio Grande Valley to as much as 300 inches in the mountains of north-central New Mexico. Several regions of the state offer fascinating studies in contrast. Southeastern New Mexico, for example, features two mountain towns, Ruidoso and Cloudcroft, that thrive as ski centers high above the dry prairie and vast desert. In between these two towns is Inn of the Mountain Gods, the state's finest and most recognized golf resort.

Golf is still in its infantile stages in New Mexico, despite the fact that the pleasant year-round temperatures, dry climate, and spectacular scenery offer the perfect golfing scenario. Those who equate New Mexico with "desert" should take in a few rounds at Inn of the Mountain Gods or Angel Fire, to get a perspective on this fascinating diversity that abounds in this state. New Mexico is truly a land of enlightenment, as well as enchantment.

Inn of the Mountain Gods

A Native American gift of stunning grandeur

THERE IS A PLACE IN SOUTH-CENTRAL New Mexico, rising some 7,000 feet into the Sacramento Mountains, which abounds in such beauty that the Mescalero Apache Indians call it their home of the Mountain Gods. Tucked into a pine-sheathed valley in the heart of the Mescalero Apache reservation, along the shore of Lake Mescalero, is the tribe's gift to the rest of the world—the aptly named Inn of the Mountain Gods.

The Inn genuinely reflects the serenity and seclusion of the 460,000-acre reservation, which was established in 1873. The resort itself was the dream of Tribal Chief Wendell Chino, who sought to create a facility that blended harmoniously with the natural beauty of the surroundings, but that also served as a vocational training ground for his people. After years of planning and political maneuvering, the Inn opened in 1975 and has successfully fulfilled Chino's wishes. The gracious and accommodating staff consists largely of tribal members, and the resort itself is both a peaceful, idyllic retreat as well as an outdoor wonderland teeming with recreational opportunities, regardless of the season.

Accommodations at the Inn consist of 250 chalet-style rooms and suites, all with private balconies offering sweeping views of the lake and the Sierra Blanca Mountains, and a seemingly abnormal amount of peace and quiet.

But things get a little livelier at night. The lobby lounge, Gos Kan Bar, with its 50-foot copper sheathed fireplace, is a convivial gathering place, and the Dan Li Ka dining room offers outstanding cuisine and a very good wine list. During the summer-fall season (June through October), the Ina Da Lounge offers dancing and live entertainment (which is actually the *only* entertainment for many miles in these parts).

Now back to the outdoors. While the skiing here is outstanding from Thanksgiving to Easter (packages and transportation to nearby slopes are available through the Inn), the summer months offer a myriad of activities that take full advantage of the setting. Not the least of which is golf, which is played on a Ted Robinson-designed, 18-hole course that has been lauded as the best in the state by several national publications. It's a rolling layout bordering Lake Mescalero, with fairways lined with stands of pinion, cottonwood, aspen and pine. The extreme elevation helps in tackling the course's length—6,819 yards from the tips, but only 6,416 from the regular tees—but the greens are large, undulating and very quick, and the lake comes into play quite often.

A good example is the par-four 10th hole, which requires a tee shot to an island fairway, followed by an approach to a large green set hard against the lake.

Unless fishing for golf balls has dampened your desire to wet a line, there are rainbow and cutthroat trout to be taken from the lake. The Inn also offers tennis, swimming, trap and skeet shooting, horseback riding (which should not be missed) and excursions to the nearby village of Ruidoso, where thoroughbred racing is the sport of choice during the summer. The true outdoorsman may want to take advantage of a big-game hunting package. After all, this is definitely where the deer and the antelope play.

And as far as I can tell about the Inn of the Mountain Gods, seldom is heard a discouraging word. ∎

Inn of the Mountain Gods
P.O. Box 269
Mescalero, NM 88340

LOCATION: 191 miles southeast of Albuquerque, N.M., 124 miles north of El Paso, Tex.

ACCOMMODATIONS: 230 rooms, 10 mini-suites and 10 parlor suites.

DINING/ENTERTAINMENT: The Dan Ki La, excellent international cuisine with fine wine list and outstanding Sunday brunch; Apache Tee Restaurant and Lounge, light fare served seasonally; Top O' The Inn, cocktail lounge with spectacular views; Gos Kan Bar, fireside lobby lounge with seasonal entertainment; Ina Da Lounge, live entertainment and dancing seasonally.

AMENITIES: 18 holes of golf (Ted Robinson); six lighted tennis courts; boating and fishing on Lake Mescalero; heated outdoor swimming pool and spa; horseback riding; trap and skeet shooting; retail shop with apparel and specialty items. Nearby (four miles) is the village of Ruidoso with galleries, boutiques, horse racing, and skiing.

MEETING FACILITIES: More than 19,000 square feet of divisible space including 6,416-square-foot Wendell Chino Ballroom.

RATES: Standard rooms from $80, mini-suites and parlors from $90 (based on availability). Golf and tennis packages available from $240.

RESERVATIONS: Call (800) 545-9011 or (505) 257-5141.

Angel Fire Resort

ANGEL FIRE, NEW MEXICO, HAS offered some of the finest, and most reasonably priced, downhill skiing in the Southwest for 26 years. Nestled in the Rocky Mountains just south of the Colorado border, Angel Fire's 8,500-foot elevation and 30 miles of trails have enabled the resort to host both the U.S. Pro Tour and the World Cup Freestyle Championships.

But summer is becoming just as popular in these parts as the winter season, thanks to a fine 18-hole golf course that ranks as one of the highest in the country. While the altitude causes the ball to fly some 20 to 30 yards further, distance is not paramount on this 6,624-yard course. With extremely rolling terrain, tight fairways lined with pine and aspen (and out-of-bounds), and water coming into play on 13 holes, the key to scoring at Angel Fire is to keep the ball in play.

The length of the course is found primarily on the back nine, which was built 10 years after the original nine and is highlighted by the 15th hole, a 225-yard par-three that plays sharply downhill. Depending on the weather, club selection at No. 15 can vary dramatically. Head professional Chris Stewart claims to have hit anywhere from a 9-iron in favorable conditions to a 5-wood on rougher days.

Angel Fire Country Club offers a large dining room and lounge area, and several attractively priced golf packages are available through the nearby Legends Hotel and Conference Center, where accommodations range from standard hotel rooms to spacious condominiums. Other available amenities include boating and fishing in two magnificent lakes, Eagle Nest and Monte Verde, as well as horseback riding, Jeep tours, tennis, or shopping and sightseeing in nearby Taos. Whatever the season, the possibilities at Angel Fire, like the northern New Mexico mountain views, are seemingly endless. ∎

Angel Fire Resort
P.O. Drawer B
Angel Fire, NM 87710

LOCATION: 22 miles east of Taos, N.M.

ACCOMMODATIONS: Hotel rooms, suites and condominiums at Legends Hotel and Conference Center.

AMENITIES: 18 holes of golf; boating; tennis; horseback riding; Jeep tours; rafting; fishing; skiing (seasonal). Dining room, lounge and 19th hole at Country Club; additional dining, entertainment and meeting facilities at Legends Hotel.

RATES: Standard hotel rooms from $55, suites from $75, condominiums from $60; golf packages available.

RESERVATIONS: Call (800) 633-7463.

Places To Play

New Mexico

Albuquerque

Arroyo del Oso Golf Course
7001 Osuna Road
Albuquerque, NM 87109
(505) 884-7505
TYPE OF FACILITY: Public
NO. OF HOLES: 27
YARDAGE: 6,892/3,350
PAR: 72/36
COMMENTS: Well-bunkered course with small greens. Tough par-threes.

University of New Mexico South Golf Course
University Boulevard SE
Albuquerque, NM 87131
(505) 277-4546
TYPE OF FACILITY: Public
NO. OF HOLES: 18
YARDAGE: 7,253
PAR: 72
COMMENTS: Long, demanding test in rugged desert terrain.

Conchiti Lake Golf Course

**Double Eagle Country
Club & Lodge**
3500 Country Club Lane NW
Albuquerque, NM 87114
(505) 898-7001
TYPE OF FACILITY: Resort
NO. OF HOLES: 18

YARDAGE: 6,098-6,895
PAR: Women 74, Men 72
COMMENTS: Paradise Hills Course
designed by Red Lawrence. Flat
terrain, numerous lakes and 80
bunkers. Part of small resort
lodge.

Las Cruces

**New Mexico State University
Golf Course**
P.O. Box 3595
Las Cruces, NM 88003
(505) 646-3219
TYPE OF FACILITY: Public
NO. OF HOLES: 18
YARDAGE: 7,040
PAR: 72
COMMENTS: Site of 1968 NCAA
Championship. All 18 holes can
be seen from the clubhouse.

Picacho Hills Country Club
6861 Via Campestre
Las Cruces, NM 88005
(505) 523-2556
TYPE OF FACILITY: Private/Reciprocal
NO. OF HOLES: 18
YARDAGE: 6,957
PAR: 72
COMMENTS: Rolling, Joe Finger-
designed course with nine lakes
and bluegrass fairways. Call pro
in advance to schedule tee time.

Conchiti Lake/Santa Fe

Conchiti Lake Golf Course
P.O. Box 125
Santa Fe, NM 87041
(505) 465-2239
TYPE OF FACILITY: Public
NO. OF HOLES: 18

YARDAGE: 6,450
PAR: 72
COMMENTS: Scenic mountain course
located on Conchiti Pueblo Indian
Reservation just outside the city of
Santa Fe.

Index A

Index B

The Wigwam (West Course)
Litchfield Park, AZ

Jay Morrish
Painted Desert Golf Course
Las Vegas, NV

TPC at Scottsdale (Scottsdale Princess)
Scottsdale, AZ
(with Tom Weiskopf)

The Boulders
Carefree, AZ

The Foothills Golf Club
Phoenix, AZ
(with Tom Weiskopf)

Troon North
Scottsdale, AZ
(with Tom Weiskopf)

Greg Nash
Sun City Vistoso Golf Club
Tucson, AZ

Superstition Springs Golf Club
Mesa, AZ

Jack Nicklaus
La Paloma Country Club
(Westin La Paloma Resort)
Tucson, AZ

Arnold Palmer/Palmer Course Design
Angel Park Golf Course
Las Vegas, NV

Arrowhead Country Club
Glendale, AZ

Scottsdale Country Club
Scottsdale, AZ

Gary Panks
Sedona Golf Resort
Oak Creek, AZ

J. Michael Poellot
Gainey Ranch Golf Club
(Hyatt Regency at Gainey Ranch)
Scottsdale, AZ

Forrest Richardson
The Pointe Resorts (South Mountain)
Phoenix, AZ

Ted Robinson
Inn of the Mountain Gods
Mescalero, NM

Ocotillo Country Club
Chandler, AZ

Arthur Jack Snyder
Marriott's Camelback Inn
(Indian Bend Course)
Scottsdale, AZ

Index C

Mobil Travel Guide
(Published Ratings for 1992)

Five Stars

Arizona
Marriott's Camelback Inn
Scottsdale, AZ

The Wigwam
Litchfield Park, AZ

Four Stars

Arizona
The Boulders
Carefree, AZ

Hyatt Regency Scottsdale
(Gainey Ranch)
Scottsdale, AZ

Arizona Biltmore
Phoenix, AZ

The Phoenician
Scottsdale, AZ

Scottsdale Princess
Scottsdale, AZ

Loews Ventana Canyon Resort
Tucson, AZ

Tucson National Resort &
Conference Center
Tucson, AZ

Westin La Paloma
Tucson, AZ

New Mexico
Inn of the Mountain Gods
Mescalero, AZ

AAA TourBook
(Published Ratings for 1992)

Five Diamonds

Arizona
The Boulders
Carefree, AZ

Marriott's Camelback Inn
Scottsdale, AZ

Scottsdale Princess
Scottsdale, AZ

Index D COMBINATIONS OF COURSES

Arizona

Arizona Biltmore (36)
Phoenix, AZ

The Boulders (36)
Carefree, AZ

Camelot Golf Club (27)
Mesa, AZ

Fairfield Flagstaff Resort (36)
Flagstaff, AZ

Hyatt Regency Scottsdale (27)
Scottsdale, AZ

Inn at McCormick Ranch (36)
Scottsdale, AZ

Marriott's Camelback Inn (36)
Scottsdale, AZ

Ocotillo Golf Club (27)
Chandler, AZ

Randolph Park Golf Courses (36)
Tucson, AZ

Rio Verde Country Club (36)
Rio Verde, AZ

Scottsdale Country Club (27)
Scottsdale, AZ

Scottsdale Princess (36)
Scottsdale, AZ

Sheraton El Conquistador Resort (45)
Tucson, AZ

Tucson National (27)
Tucson, AZ

Ventana Canyon Golf &
Racquet Club (36)
Tucson, AZ

Westin La Paloma (27)
Tucson, AZ

The Wigwam (54)
Litchfield Park, AZ

Nevada

Incline Village Golf Course (36)
Incline Village, NV

New Mexico

Arroyo del Oso Golf Course (27)
Albuquerque, NM

Index F CHILDREN'S ACTIVITIES/PROGRAMS

Arizona
Arizona Biltmore
Phoenix, AZ

Arizona Golf Resort
Mesa, AZ

Hyatt Regency Scottsdale
(Gainey Ranch)
Scottsdale, AZ

Marriott's Camelback Inn
Scottsdale, AZ

Scottsdale Princess
Scottsdale, AZ

The Phoenician
Scottsdale, AZ

The Pointe Resorts
Phoenix, AZ

The Wigwam
Litchfield Park, AZ

Westin La Paloma
Tucson, AZ

New Mexico
Angel Fire Resort
Angel Fire, NM